illustrated index to traditional american Quilt patterns

Susan Winter Mills

ARCO PUBLISHING, INC.
NEW YORK

To Sally and Stephen

Special thanks to Joe Giardinelli
for stressing the importance of detail

Second Printing, 1981

Published by Arco Publishing, Inc.
219 Park Avenue South, New York, N.Y. 10003

Copyright © 1980 by Susan Winter Mills

Library of Congress Cataloging in Publication Data

Mills, Susan Winter.
   Illustrated index to traditional American quilt patterns.

   Includes index.
   1. Quilting—United States—Patterns.   I. Title.
TT835.M54   745.4'6   79-17147

ISBN 0-668-04777-1   Library Edition
ISBN 0-668-04782-8   Paper Edition

Printed in the United States of America

FOREWORD

Favorite of the Peruvians, Wind Power of the Osages, Chinese 10,000 Perfections, Pure Symbol of the Right Doctrine, Battle Ax of Thor, Catch Me If You Can, Heart's Seal, Mound Builders—all names for one quilt pattern; scraps of folk poetry for the pieced-work folk art that, nurtured by necessity, flourished in pre-industrial America.

Quiltmakers were prodigiously inventive—710 quilt designs are compiled herein. They showed a remarkable sense of design and an intuitive grasp of geometrics. As many of the more popular designs spread with the settling of the nation and were repropagated in new soil, they sprang up with new names; the homogenization of language by national media was still far down the road.

My intention when I began compiling patterns was to piece together a reference tool for my own quiltmaking—something to thumb through, like a catalog, a method more conducive to inspiration than going through many books.

At first, the name for each pattern was just that—a name. After poring through the sources and finding the same pattern with different names, their profusion and poetry caught my attention. As I go through the pages now, the names delight me as much as the patterns.

Quilts warmed the Bible Belt: Tents of Armageddon, Job's Tears, Garden of Eden, Ecclesiastical.

Some names are memorials to the birth of the nation and history in the making: Burgoyne Surrounded, Underground Railroad, Sherman's March, Trail of the Covered Wagon, and Free Trade Block.

More mundane events were part of the naming. We can imagine a quiltmaker coming up with Climbing Rose after a satisfying day in the garden, or an accident in the kitchen resulting in Broken Dishes.

Individuals were honored in the naming, too: Martha Washington Star, Barbara Frietchie Star, Lincoln's Platform, and Tippecanoe and Tyler Too.

Many whimsical names were evoked by the patterns: Duck's Foot in the Mud, Pickle Dish, Drunkard's Path, and Wild Goose Chase.

Sister's Choice, Granny's Garden, Aunt Eliza's Star, Mother's Fancy Star, and Baby Bunting all reflect the importance of family; Always Friends, Nextdoor Neighbor, and Friendship Chain echo the warmth of companionship.

To put a practical face on it, collecting as many names as possible is the only sensible way to index patterns that may be known by different names in adjacent counties. In laying out the book, it was necessary to choose one "main" name for each pattern as they were arranged in sections, with secondary names for the pattern listed below the primary name. All names are included in the index to facilitate a pattern search by the reader. If the name for a quilt pattern is the object of the search, the patterns have been arranged in sections according, more or less, to the most prevalent geometric figure. (Some patterns were difficult to classify—they could easily have fallen as well into one classification as another—so I clenched my teeth and surrendered to pure arbitrariness.) After deciding what shape—triangle, square, circle, star, or combination—is predominant in your quilt, you need only thumb through that section until you recognize the pattern.

Since quilt patterns depend on the juxtaposition of light and dark fabric to bring out the design, the illustrations in this book are rendered in black and white. A quiltmaker can find a pattern he or she likes, count the shades therein, assign corresponding shades of fabric, and be assured that the quilt he makes will be a faithful rendering of the pattern.

With many patterns, using different color schemes can cause a subject-field shift or otherwise completely change the aspect of the quilt, making it hard to apprehend how it is put together. Like a blueprint, renderings of patterns in black and white bring up the details relevant to construction.

The patterns were drafted on a five-to-an-inch grid. Overlaying patterns with tracing paper with the same grid provides a unit measure for the pattern. Dividing the projected dimensions of the quilt by the number of units will indicate the size of individual blocks and pieces of the block.

Templates can then be cut to the appropriate sizes and used to trace the pieces on fabric. I cut about ¼ inch beyond and stitch on top of the traced line.

Because of their strong graphic sense, quilt patterns may be adapted for use in many areas of arts and crafts. (Z-Cross contains four figures identical to the NBC-TV logo.) Designs can also be utilized in other textile crafts such as weaving, needlepoint, and embroidery.

After I sent these patterns to the publisher, an article I wrote for my hometown paper prompted a letter from a reader with a query about and sketches of two patterns. One was among the 710 compiled here, but the other was not. I realized that the book will probably generate enough new sources and patterns to provide a diversion for many years to come.

CONTENTS

Stars

Alice's Favorite

Arkansas Traveller
Travel Star

All Hallows

Aunt Eliza's Star

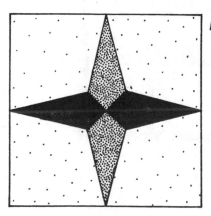

Arkansas Snowflake
Four-Point
Job's Troubles, Var. 2
Kite
Snowball, Var. 3

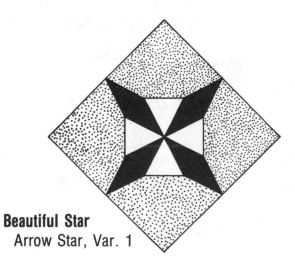

Beautiful Star
Arrow Star, Var. 1

Blazing Star Variation 1

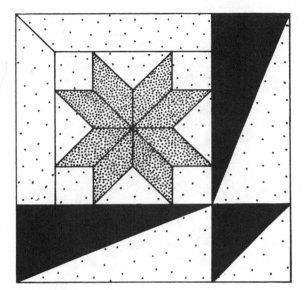

Bouquet in a Fan

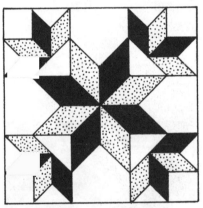

Blazing Star Variation 2
Lemon Star, Var. 3

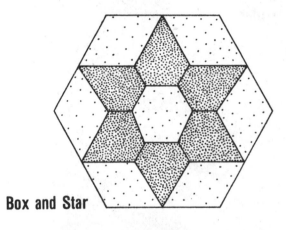

Box and Star

Blazing Sun

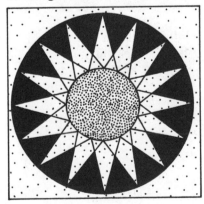

Caesar's Crown

California Star Variation 1

Carpenter's Wheel Variation 2

California Star Variation 2

Chained Star
Brunswick Star, Var. 1
Rolling Star, Var. 3

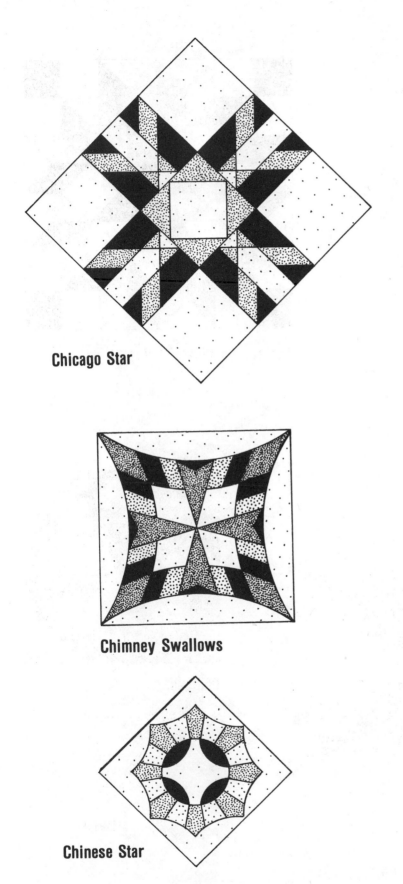

Chicago Star

Chimney Swallows

Chinese Star

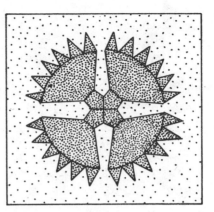

Chips and Whetstones
Variation 1

Chips and Whetstones
Variation 2

Chips and Whetstones
Variation 3

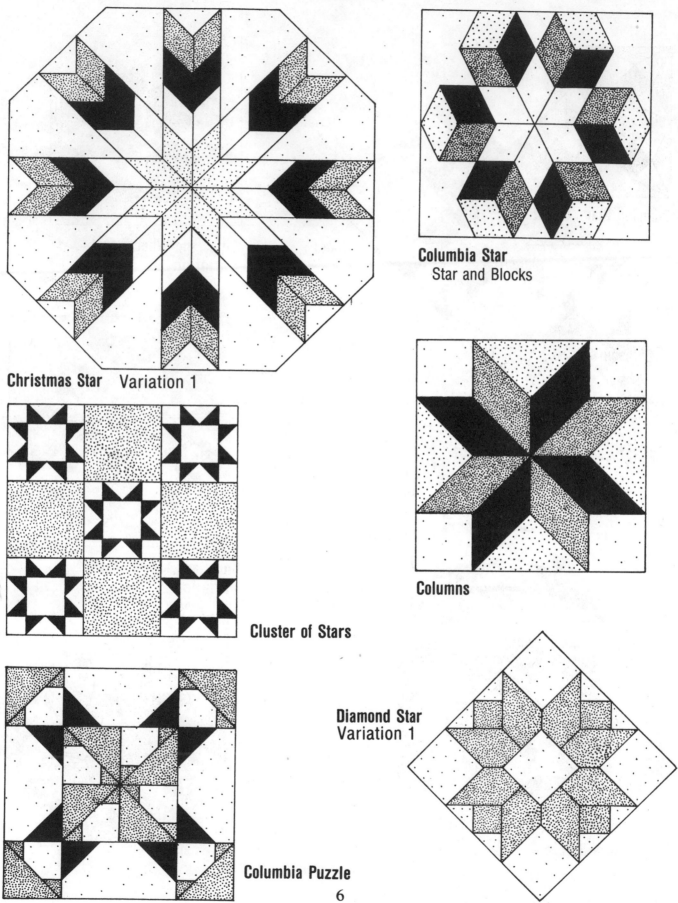

Christmas Star Variation 1

Columbia Star
Star and Blocks

Cluster of Stars

Columns

Diamond Star
Variation 1

Columbia Puzzle

6

Diamond Star Variation 2

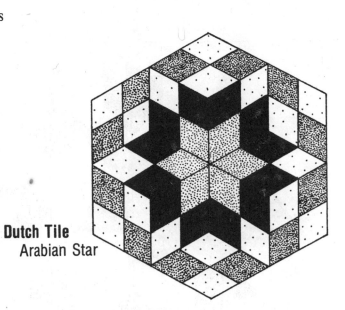

Dutch Tile
Arabian Star

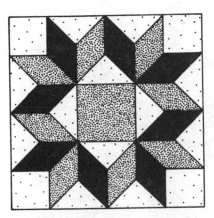

Dove at the Window

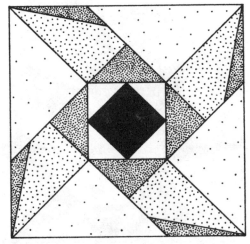

Eccentric Star Variation 2

Dutch Rose
Octagonal Star, Var. 1

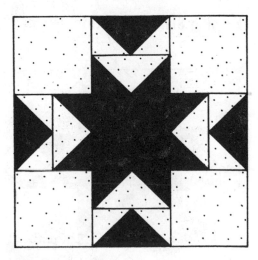

Eight-Pointed Star Variation 2

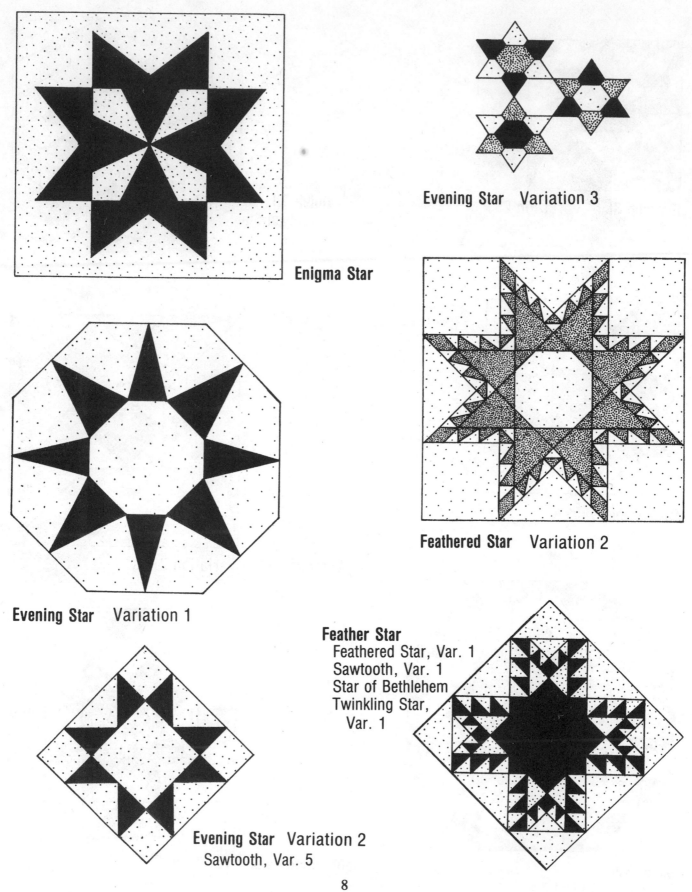

Enigma Star

Evening Star   Variation 3

Feathered Star   Variation 2

Evening Star   Variation 1

Evening Star   Variation 2
Sawtooth, Var. 5

Feather Star
Feathered Star, Var. 1
Sawtooth, Var. 1
Star of Bethlehem
Twinkling Star,
    Var. 1

8

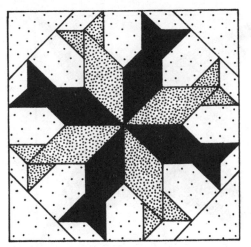

Fish Block
  Goldfish

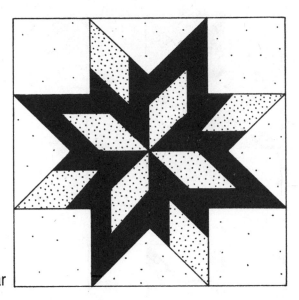

Flying Bat
  Polaris Star

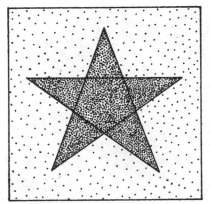

Five-Pointed Star

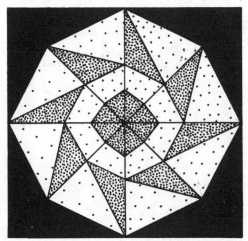

Flying Saucer

Flower Star   Variation 1

Flying Swallow
  Circling Swallows
  Falling Star
  Flying Star

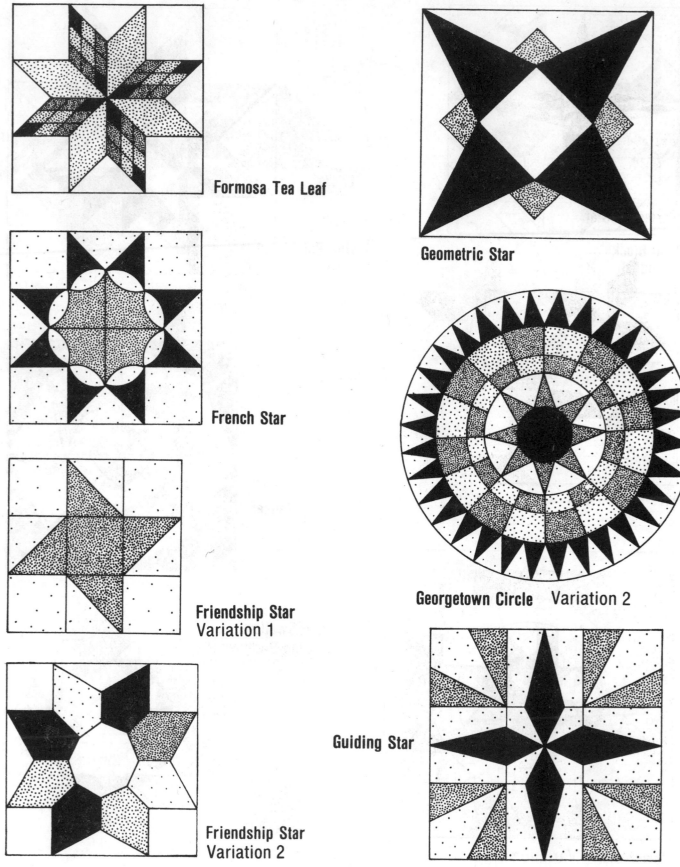

Formosa Tea Leaf

Geometric Star

French Star

Georgetown Circle   Variation 2

Friendship Star
Variation 1

Guiding Star

Friendship Star
Variation 2

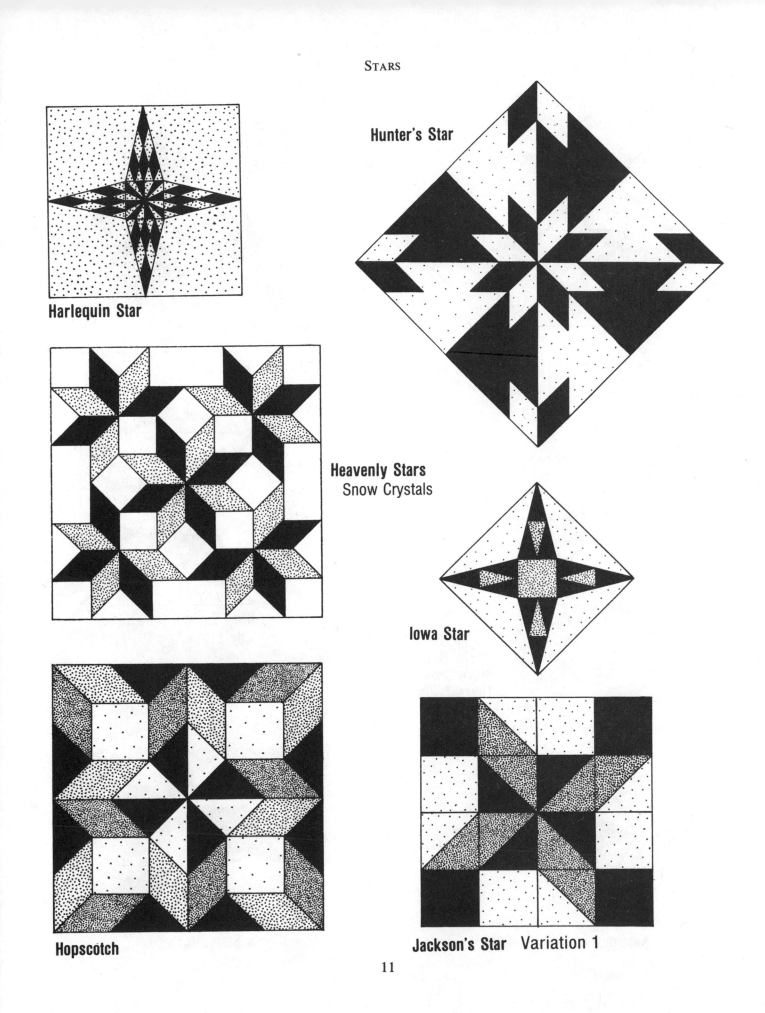

Harlequin Star

Hunter's Star

Heavenly Stars
Snow Crystals

Iowa Star

Hopscotch

Jackson's Star Variation 1

11

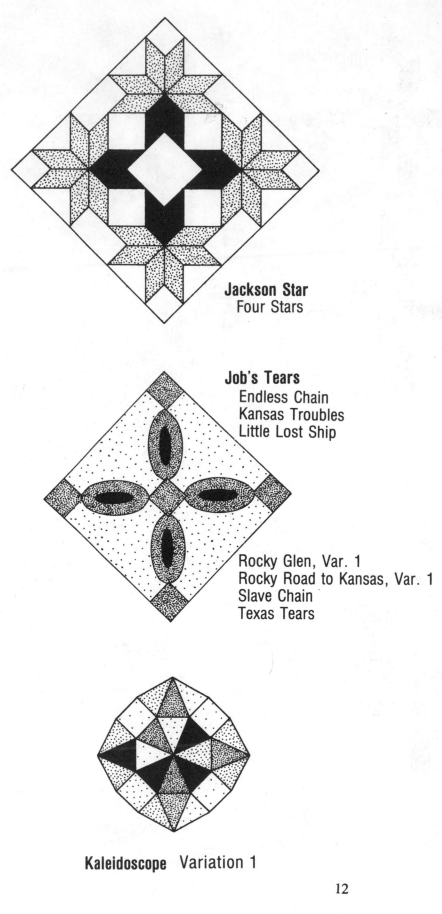

Jackson Star
Four Stars

Job's Tears
Endless Chain
Kansas Troubles
Little Lost Ship

Rocky Glen, Var. 1
Rocky Road to Kansas, Var. 1
Slave Chain
Texas Tears

Kaleidoscope Variation 1

Key West Star

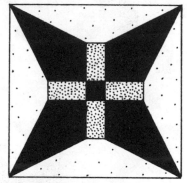

King David's Crown
Variation 1

King's Star Variation 1

12

Lazy Daisy   Variation 2

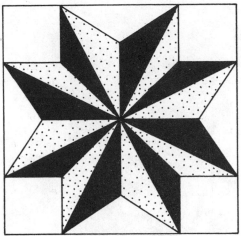

Le Moyne Star   Variation 2
   Divided Star
   Lemon Star, Var. 2
   Star of LeMoine, Var. 2
   Star of LeMoyne, Var. 2

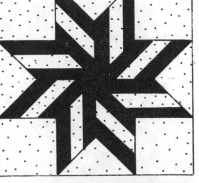

Liberty Star

Light and Shadows

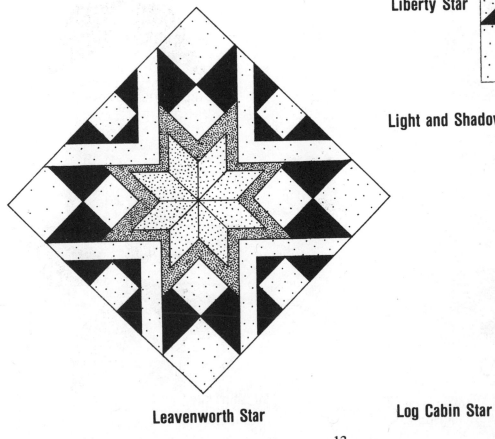

Leavenworth Star

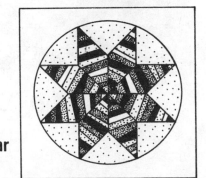

Log Cabin Star

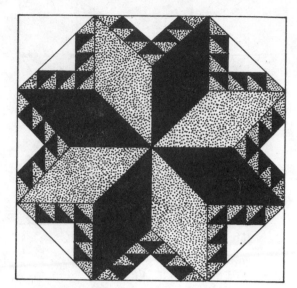

Lucinda's Star

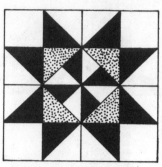

Martha Washington Star

Many-pointed Star

Mexican Rose
Mexican Star, Var. 1

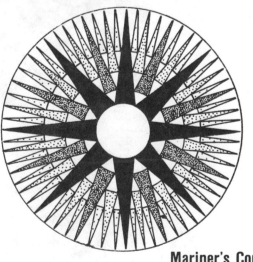

Mariner's Compass
Rising Sun, Var. 1

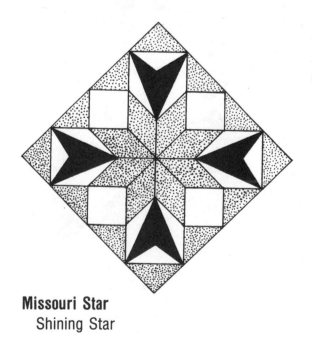

Missouri Star
Shining Star

14

Modern Star

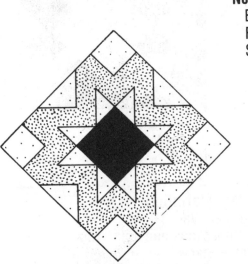

Morning Star   Variation 1

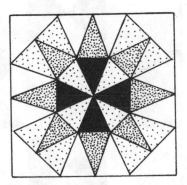

Morning Star   Variation 2

Northern Lights
Blazing Star, Var. 3
Four-Pointed Star
Star, Var. 2

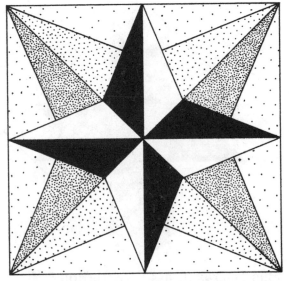

Morning Star   Variation 3

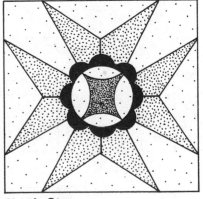

North Star
Star Tulip, Var. 2

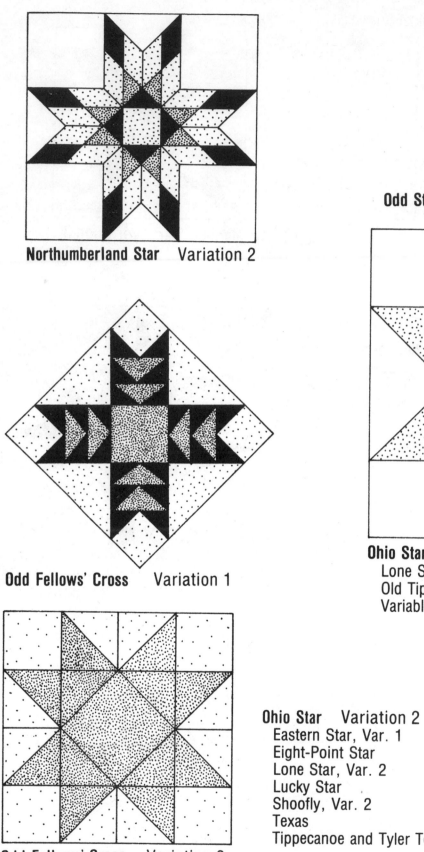

Northumberland Star   Variation 2

Odd Fellows' Cross   Variation 1

Odd Fellows' Cross   Variation 2

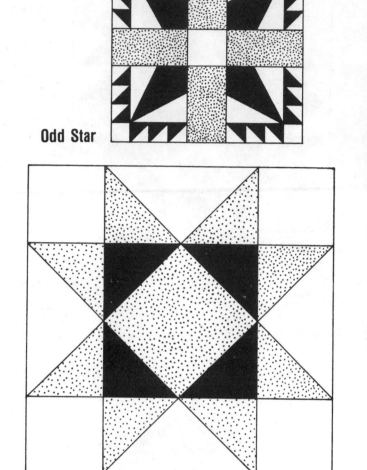

Odd Star

Ohio Star   Variation 1
Lone Star, Var. 1
Old Tippecanoe and Tyler Too
Variable Star

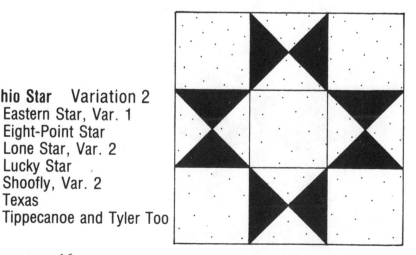

Ohio Star   Variation 2
Eastern Star, Var. 1
Eight-Point Star
Lone Star, Var. 2
Lucky Star
Shoofly, Var. 2
Texas
Tippecanoe and Tyler Too

16

Oklahoma Star
Rising Sun, Var. 2

Ozark Star
Ozark Diamond

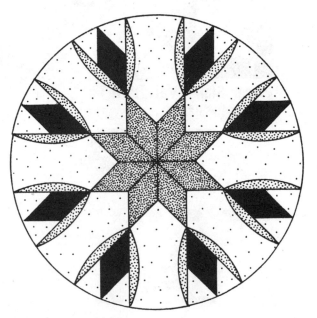

Olive's Yellow Tulip

Patty's Star

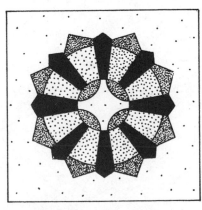

Oriental Star   Variation 1

Persian Star

Pieced Star   Variation 1
Pierced Star

Pointing Star

Philippines

Pontiac Star

Purple Cross

Prairie Queen
Variation 2

Prairie Star
   Harvest Star
   Harvest Sun
   Ship's Wheel

Queen of the May

Ring Around the Star
   Rolling Star, Var. 2
   Star and Chains

19

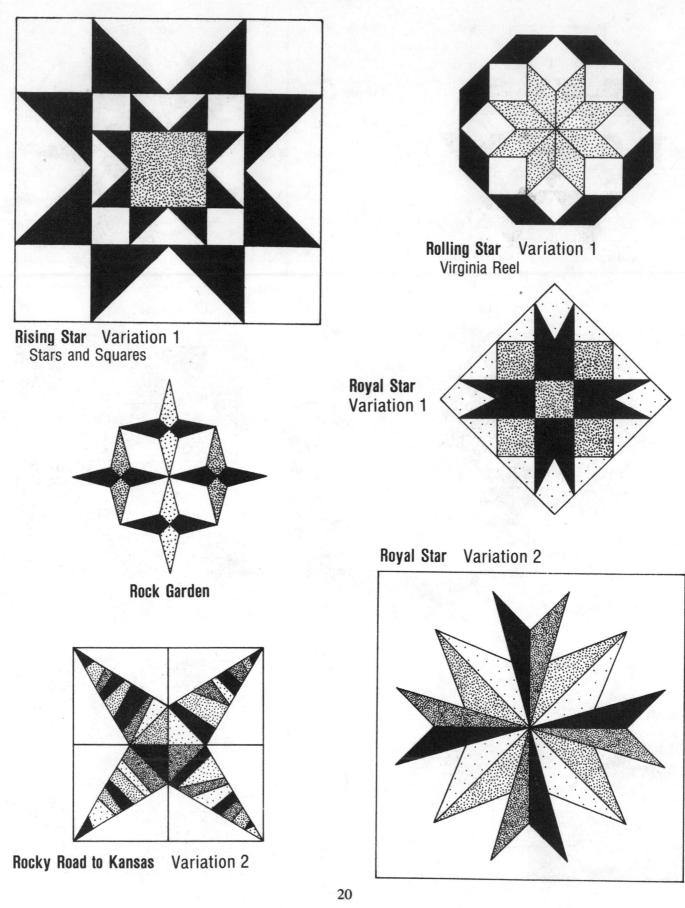

Rising Star Variation 1
Stars and Squares

Rolling Star Variation 1
Virginia Reel

Royal Star
Variation 1

Rock Garden

Royal Star Variation 2

Rocky Road to Kansas Variation 2

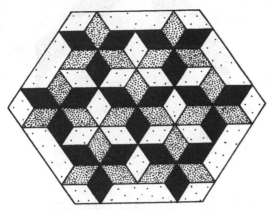

Seven Sisters
Evening Star, Var. 4

Slashed Star
Sunflower

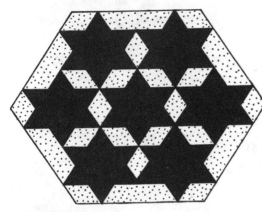

Seven Stars
Boutonniere

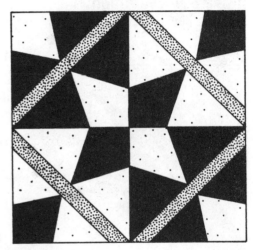

Small Business

Sky Rocket

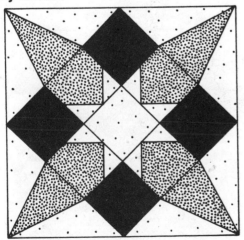

Spiderweb
Variation 2

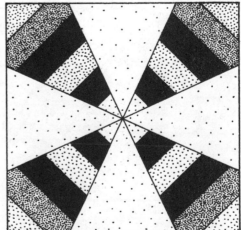

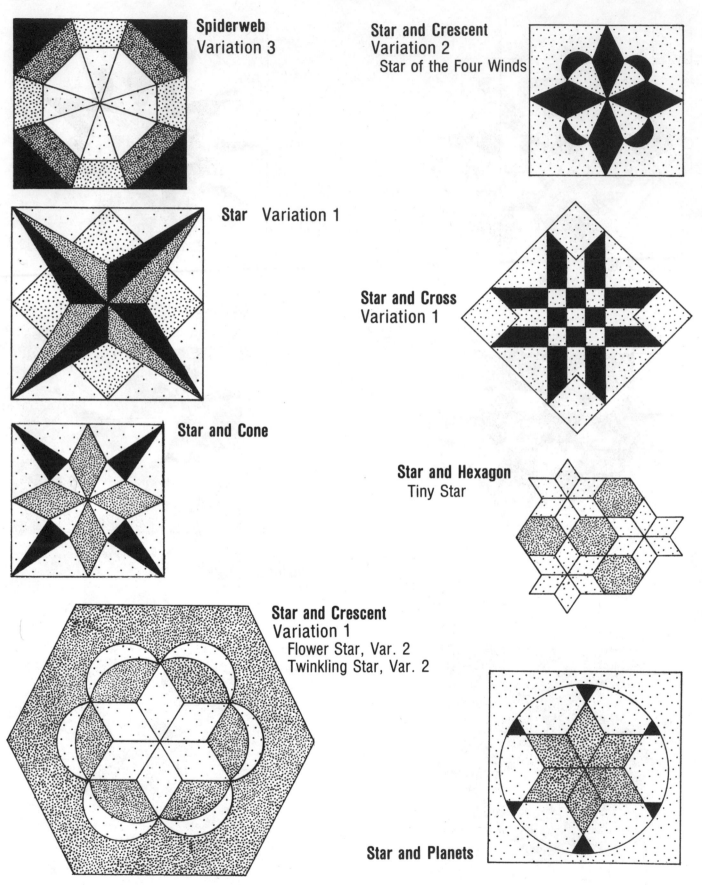

Spiderweb
Variation 3

Star and Crescent
Variation 2
Star of the Four Winds

Star Variation 1

Star and Cross
Variation 1

Star and Cone

Star and Hexagon
Tiny Star

Star and Crescent
Variation 1
Flower Star, Var. 2
Twinkling Star, Var. 2

Star and Planets

Star Flower
Variation 2

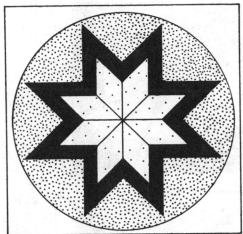

Star of Hope
Variation 2

Starlight   Variation 1

Star of Le Moyne   Variation 1
    Brunswick Star, Var. 2
    Eight-Pointed Star,
      Var. 1
    Lemon Star, Var. 1
    LeMoyne Star, Var. 1
    Star of the East, Var. 1
    Star of LeMoine, Var. 1

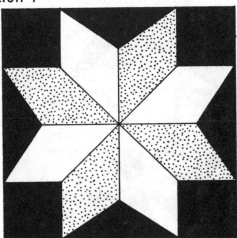

Starlight
Variation 2

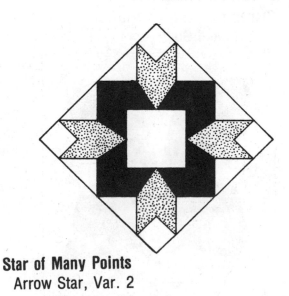

Star of Many Points
Arrow Star, Var. 2

23

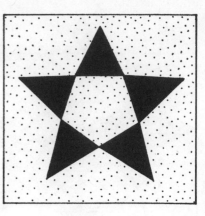

Star of the West
Variation 2

Star of North Carolina
North Carolina Star

Star of the East   Variation 3
Silver and Gold

St. Louis Star
Variation 1

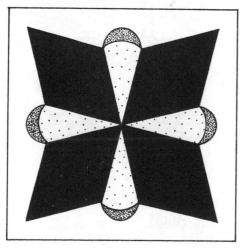

Star of the West
Variation 1
 Compass, Var. 1
 Four Birds
 Four Winds
 King's Star, Var. 2

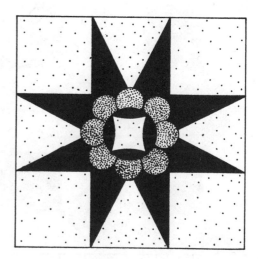

Star Tulip
Variation 1

Sunburst
Variation 1

Star Within a Star
   Carpenter's Wheel, Var. 1
   Double Star
   Star of the East, Var. 2

String Quilt

Sunburst   Variation 2

Sunbeam

Sunburst   Variation 3

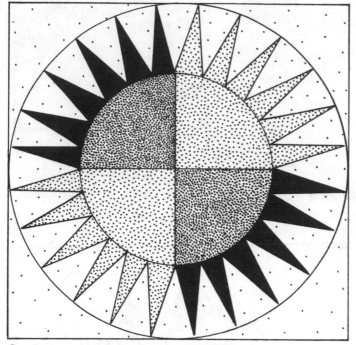

Sunburst   Variation 4

Swallows in a Window

Tennessee Star

Tangled Cobwebs

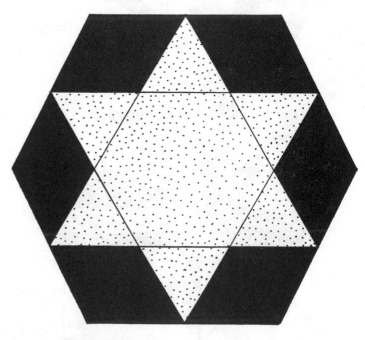

Texas Star

Union Star

Yankee Pride
Maple Leaf, Var. 3

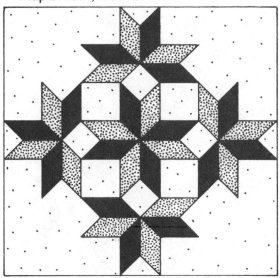

Virginia Star
Eastern Star, Var. 2
Star upon Stars
Virginia's Star

SUPPLEMENT

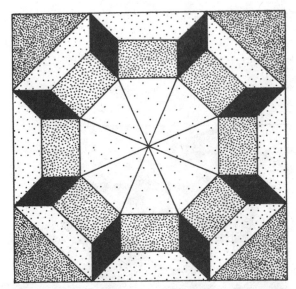

Castle Wall

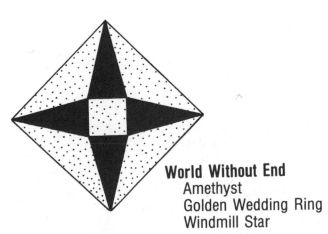

World Without End
Amethyst
Golden Wedding Ring
Windmill Star

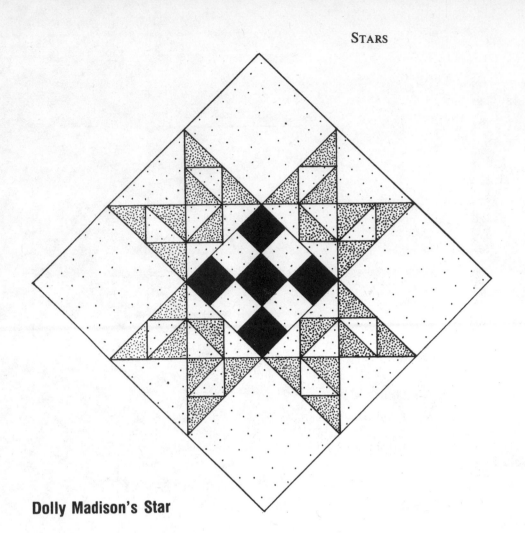

Dolly Madison's Star

Eight-Pointed Star Variation 3

Triangles

Aircraft

Barbara Frietchie Star
Star Puzzle

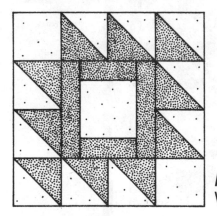

Album
Variation 4

Barn Raising

Album
Variation 5

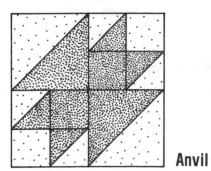

Anvil

Barrister's Block
Lawyer's Puzzle

Basket of Triangles
Fruit Basket, Var. 2

Birds in Air
Variation 3

Birds in Air   Variation 1
Flying Birds
Flying Geese, Var. 1
Flock of Geese

Blindman's Fancy

Birds in Air   Variation 2

Bow

31

Boxes
Variation 2

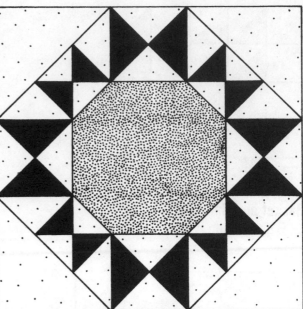

Buttons and Bows
Wheel of Fortune, Var. 3

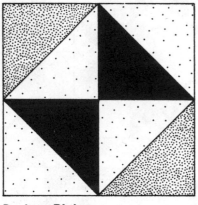

Broken Dishes

Cactus Flower

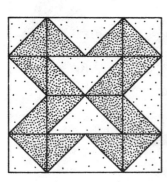

Brown Goose
　　Brown
　　Devil's Claws, Var. 1
　　Double Z
　　Grey Goose

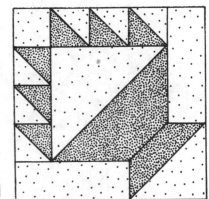

Cakestand

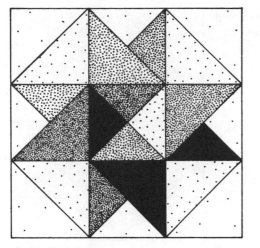

Card Trick

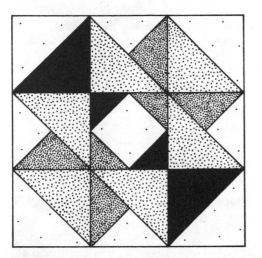

Castle in Air

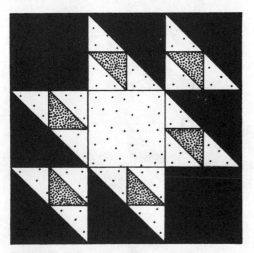

Cat's Cradle

Century
Variation 2

Cherry Basket Variation 1
Flower Basket

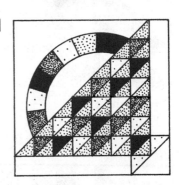

Cherry Basket
Variation 2

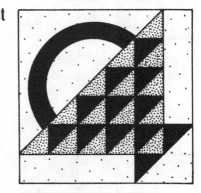

Christmas Tree
Tree of Life, Var. 3

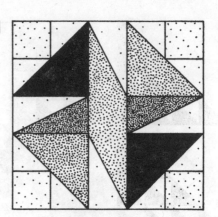

Crazy Ann Variation 1
Follow the Leader
Twist and Turn

City Square
London Square

Corn and Beans
Variation 2
    Duck and Duckling
    Handy Andy, Var. 4
    Hen and Chickens, Var. 1
    Shoofly, Var. 4

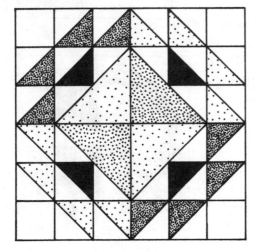

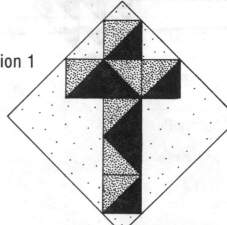

Cross
Variation 1

Crossed Canoes
    Tippecanoe

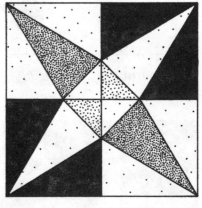

Cotton Reel

Crosses and Losses
    Double X, Var. 2
    Fox and Geese
    Old Maid's Puzzle
    X

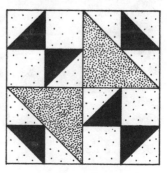

Double Pyramid

Dove in the Window   Variation 1

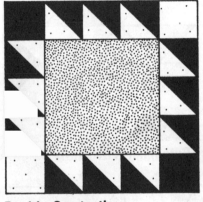

Double Sawtooth

Duck and Ducklings
 Corn and Beans, Var. 1
 Handy Andy, Var. 5
 Hens and Chickens, Var. 1
 Shoofly, Var. 3
 Wild Goose Chase, Var. 2

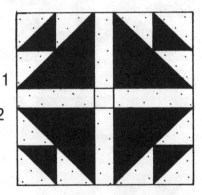

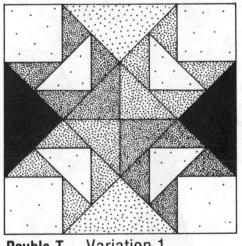

Double T   Variation 1

Dutchman's Puzzle
 Dutch Windmill

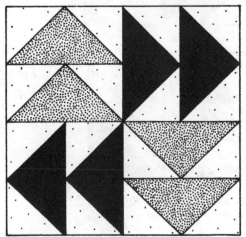

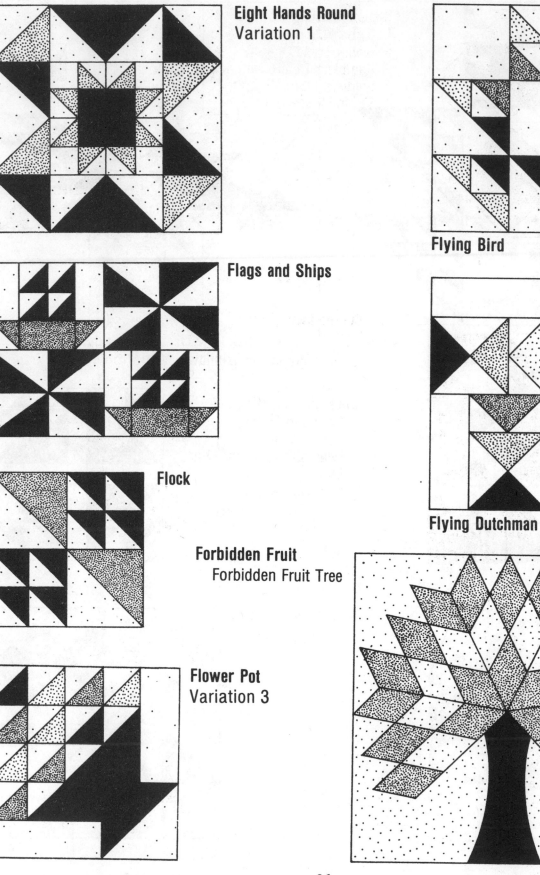

Eight Hands Round
Variation 1

Flying Bird

Flags and Ships

Flying Dutchman Variation 3

Flock

Forbidden Fruit
Forbidden Fruit Tree

Flower Pot
Variation 3

36

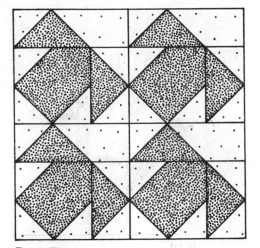

Four Ts
  Mixed T

Geese in Flight
  Battlegrounds
  Indian Trails, Var. 2
  Rambling Road, Var. 2
  Soldiers March
  Storm at Sea, Var. 3

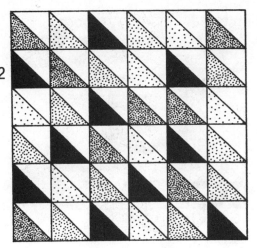

Four X

Georgetown Circles

Fruit Basket   Variation 1

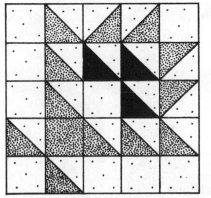

Golden Stairs

37

Goose in the Pond
Variation 1

Gretchen

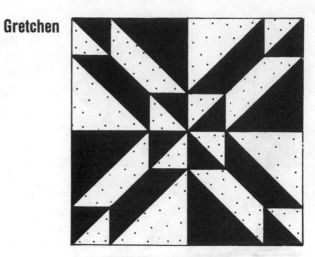

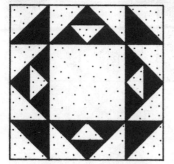

Grandmother's Favorite

Handy Andy Variation 1
Gentleman's Fancy

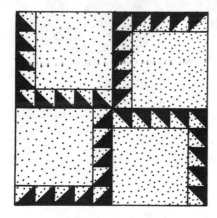

Grandmother's Pinwheel

Hill and Valley

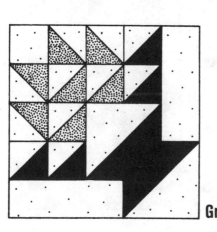

Grape Basket

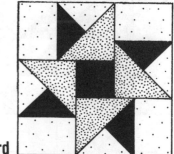

Hope of Hartford

38

Hovering Birds

Ice Cream Bowl

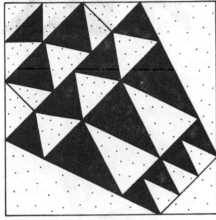

Indian Trails
Variation 1

Bear's Paw, Var. 2
Climbing Rose
Flying Dutchman, Var. 2
Forest Path
Irish Puzzle
Kansas Trouble, Var. 1
North Wind, Var. 1
Old Maid's Ramble, Var. 1
Prickly Pear, Var. 2

Rambling Road, Var. 1
Rambling Rose
Storm at Sea, Var. 1
Tangled Tares
Weather Vane, Var. 1
Winding Walk

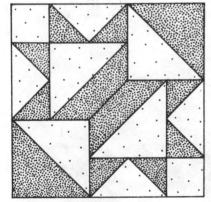

Indian Meadows
Variation 2
Queen Charlotte's Crown, Var. 2

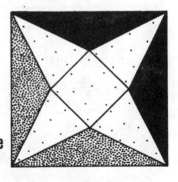

Kaleidoscope
Variation 2

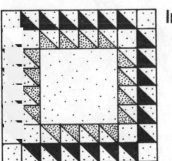

Indian Plumes

Kaleidoscope
Variation 3

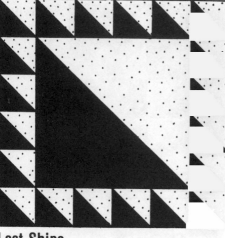

Lost Ships
 Lady of the Lake, Var. 2
 Rockly Glen, Var. 2

Kansas Trouble Variation 2

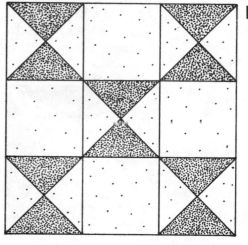

Letter X
 Clown's Choice
 Flying X

Maltese Cross
Variation 1

Maryland Beauty

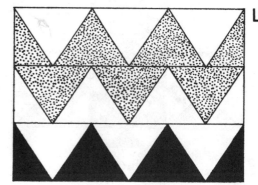

Lightning Strips
 Chevron
 Rail Fence
 Snake Fence, Var. 1
 Streak of Lightning
 Zigzag, Var. 1
 1,000 Pyramids

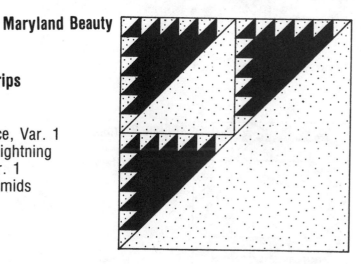

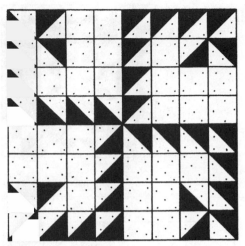

Merry Go Round

New York Beauty Variation 2
Rocky Mountain Road

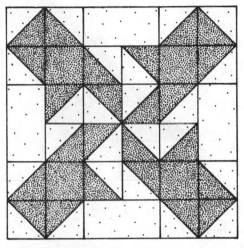

Mrs. Morgan's Choice

Next-door Neighbor

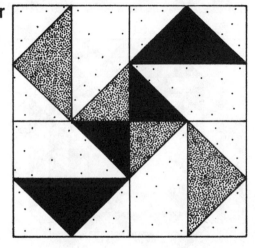

Night and Day

New York Beauty
Variation 1

North Wind
Variation 2

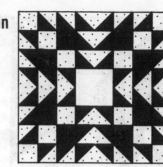

Odd Fellows' Chain

Ocean Waves
Variation 1

Old Maid's Ramble
Variation 2
    Lady of the Lake,
      Var. 1

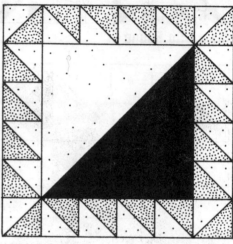

Ocean Waves
Variation 2

Old Maid's Ramble Variation 3
    Crimson Rambler
    Rambler
    Spring Beauty

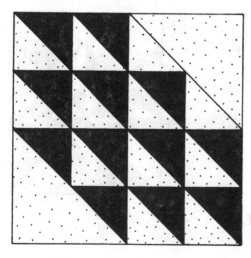

Ocean Waves
Variation 3

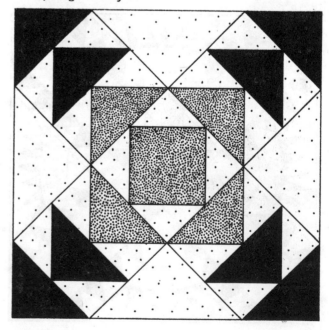

Old Maid's Ramble
Variation 4
    Lady of the Lake, Var. 3

Path Through the Woods

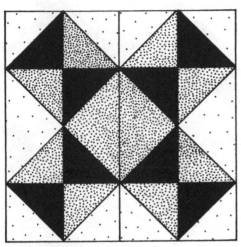

Old Tippecanoe

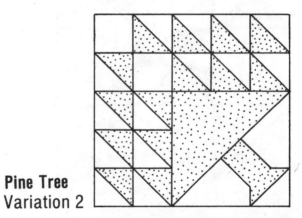

Pine Tree
Variation 2

Palm Leaves Hosannah!
    Hosanna
    Palm
    Palm Leaf, Var. 1

Pine Tree   Variation 3
    Temperance Tree, Var. 2

Pine Tree
Variation 4

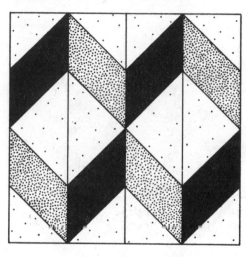

Ribbon Border

Ribbons

Pinwheel Star

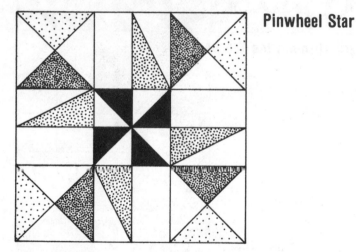

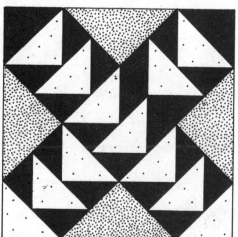

Railroad Crossing
Variation 1

Rolling Pinwheel
Variation 1

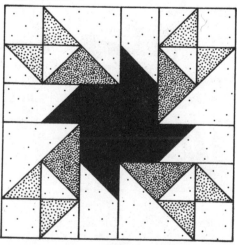

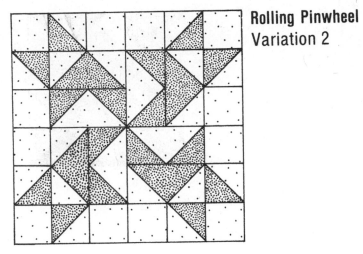

**Rolling Pinwheel
Variation 2**

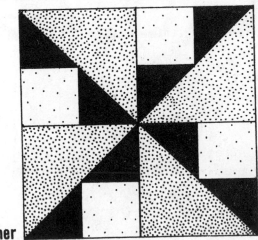

Sailboats

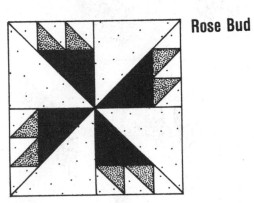

Rose Bud

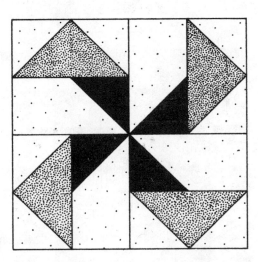

Seesaw

Sailboat

Spinner

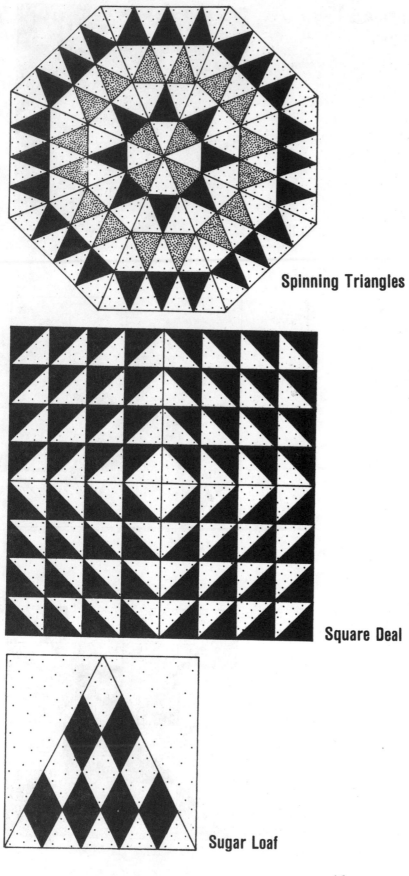

Spinning Triangles

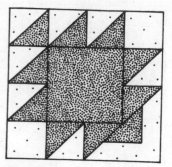

Swallow

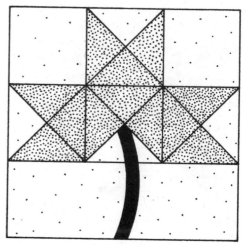

Sweet Gum Leaf

Square Deal

Sugar Loaf

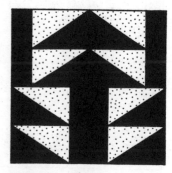

Tall Pine Tree

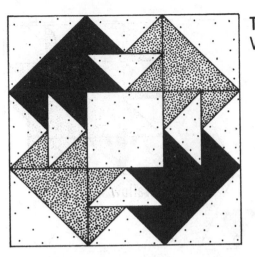

T-Blocks
Variation 1
   Capital T
   Double-T, Var. 2

Thousand Pyramids
   Pyramids
   Triangles

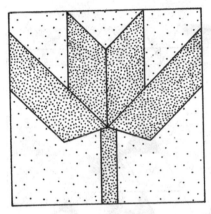

Tea Leaf
Variation 1

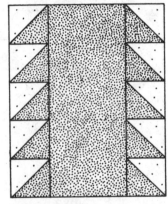

Tree of Life
Variation 2

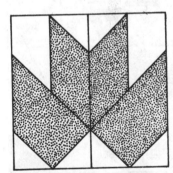

Tea Leaf
Variation 2

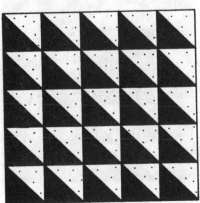

Tents of Armageddon

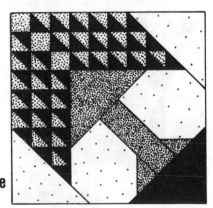

Tree of Paradise
Variation 1

47

**Tree of Paradise
Variation 2**

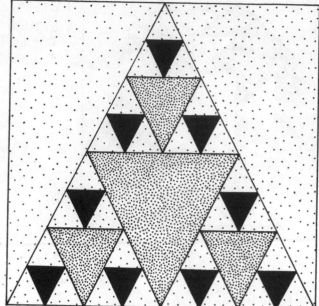

Triangular Triangles

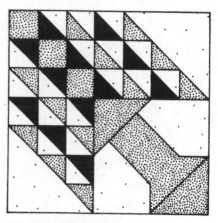

**Tree of Paradise
Variation 3**

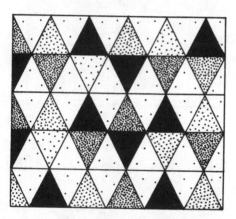

**Tumblers
Variation 1**

Triangle Puzzle

Twenty-four Triangles

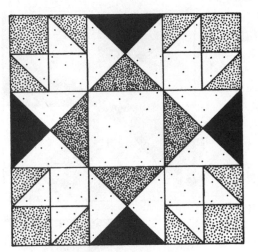

Union Squares

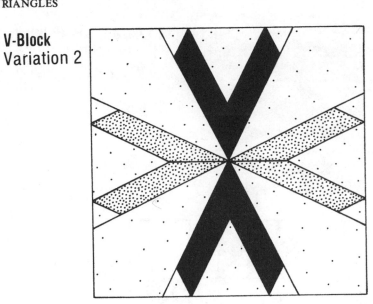

V-Block
Variation 2

Unknown Four-Patch

Water Wheel
Variation 2
Whirlwind

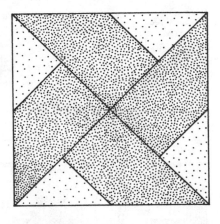

Whirligig
Variation 2

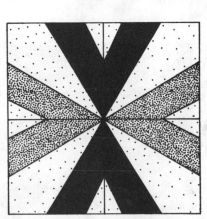

V-Block   Variation 1

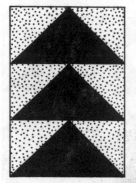

Wild Goose Chase
Variation 1

Windmill Variation 1
Crow's Foot, Var. 3
Fan Mill, Var. 1
Flutter Wheels, Var. 1
Fly, Var. 1
Honey's Choice
Kathy's Ramble, Var. 1
Mill Wheel, Var. 1
Old Windmill
Pinwheel, Var. 1
Slash Diagonal
Sugar Bowl, Var. 1
Water Mill
Water Wheel, Var. 1

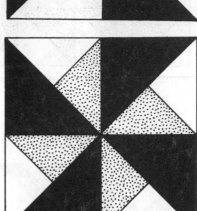

Wild Goose Chase
Variation 4

Windmill
Variation 4

Wild Goose Chase
Variation 5

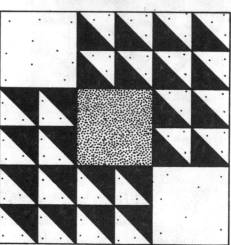

Winged Square
Variation 1
Cut Glass Dish
Golden Gates

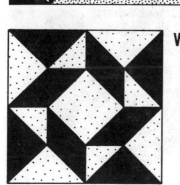

Windblown Square
Balkan Puzzle
Zigzag Tile

Yankee Puzzle
Variation 1
Hourglass, Var. 2

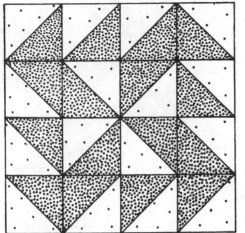

Yankee Puzzle
Variation 2

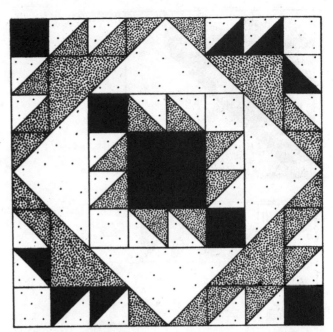

Indian Hatchet

SUPPLEMENT

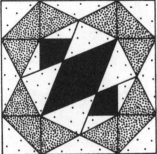

Dove in the Window Variation 2

Rocky Glen
Variation 4
Lost Ships

Free Trade
Block

Sawtooth
Variation 2

51

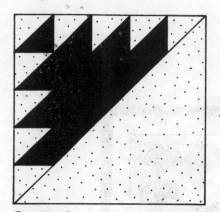

Sawtooth
Variation 4

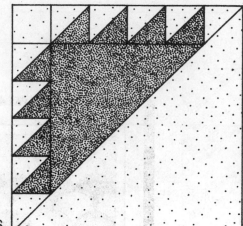

Sawtooth
Variation 6

Circles

Around the World

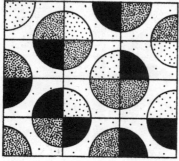

Baby Bunting

Baseball

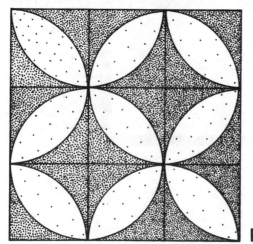

Bay Leaf

Buttercup
  Robbing Peter to
    Pay Paul, Var. 6
  Wheel of Mystery
  Winding Ways

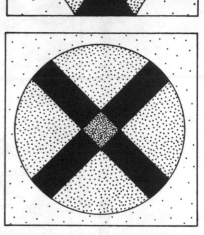

Circle Cross

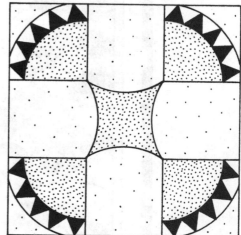

Circular Saw
  Four Little Fans
  Oriole Window

Clamshell

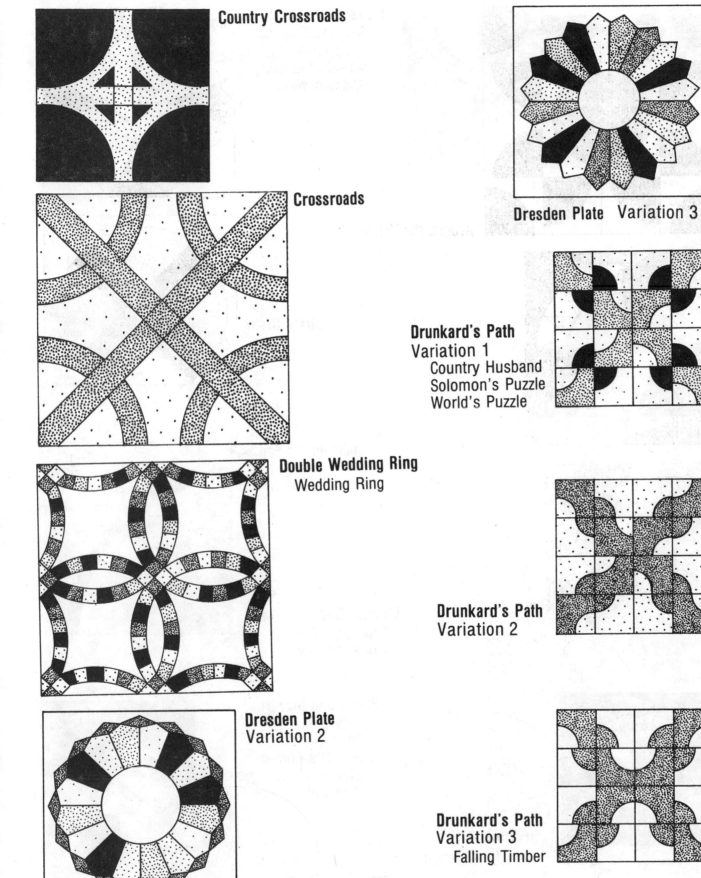

Country Crossroads

Crossroads

Double Wedding Ring
Wedding Ring

Dresden Plate
Variation 2

Dresden Plate   Variation 3

Drunkard's Path
Variation 1
    Country Husband
    Solomon's Puzzle
    World's Puzzle

Drunkard's Path
Variation 2

Drunkard's Path
Variation 3
    Falling Timber

Drunkard's Path   Variation 4

Friendship Ring
Aster
Dresden Plate,
Var. 1

Flo's Fan

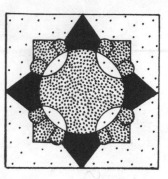

Full-blown Tulip
Variation 2

Fool's Puzzle
Variation 1

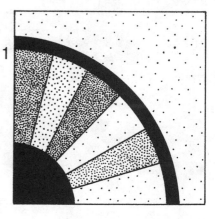

Grandmother's Fan
Fan
Fanny's Fan, Var. 1

Fool's Puzzle
Variation 2

Hearts and Gizzards
Lazy Daisy, Var. 1
Petal Quilt
Pierrot's Pom-pon
Springtime Blossom
Wheel of Fortune, Var. 1
Windmill, Var. 2

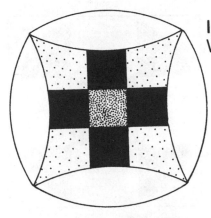

Improved Nine-patch
Variation 1
    Bailey Nine-Patch
    Glorified Nine-Patch

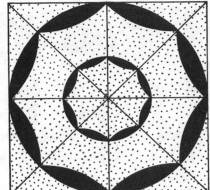

Odds and Ends

Lafayette Orange Peel
    Melon Patch
    Orange Peel, Var. 2

Love Ring
    Lone Ring
    Nonesuch

Orange Peel
Variation 1

    Compass, Var. 1
    Dolly Madison's Workbox, Var. 2
    Robbing Peter to Pay Paul, Var. 4

Missouri Beauty

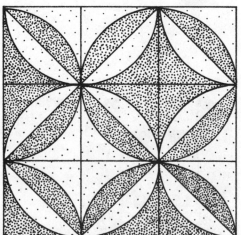

Orange Peel
Variation 3
    Dolly Madison's Workbox, Var. 1
    Rob Peter to Pay Paul, Var. 2

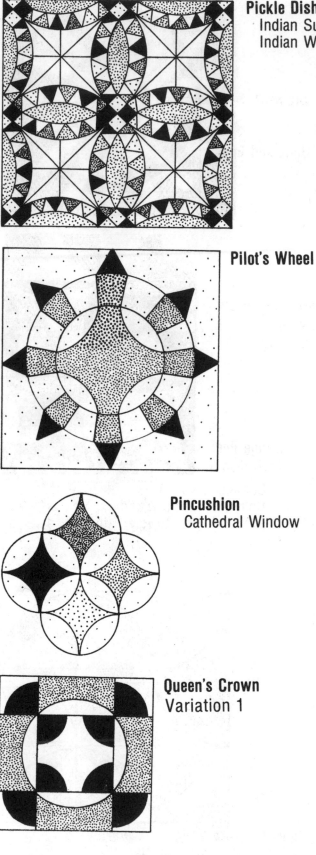

Pickle Dish
Indian Summer
Indian Wedding Ring

Pilot's Wheel

Pincushion
Cathedral Window

Queen's Crown
Variation 1

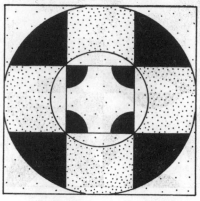

Queen's Crown
Variation 2

Queen's Pride

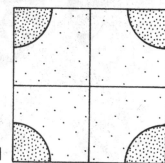

Rebecca's Fan

Reverse Baseball

Robbing Peter to Pay Paul
Variation 2

Signature

Robbing Peter to Pay Paul
Variation 3
    Falling Timbers
    Vine of Friendship

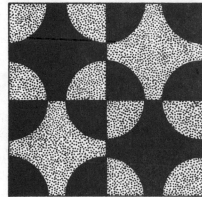

Snowball   Variation 1
    Mill Wheel, Var. 2
    Old Mill Wheel
    Pullman Puzzle

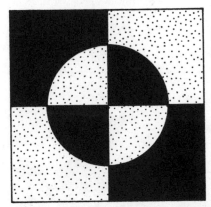

Rob Peter to Pay Paul
Variation 1

Snowball Variation 2
    Compass, Var. 3

Rocky Road to Dublin

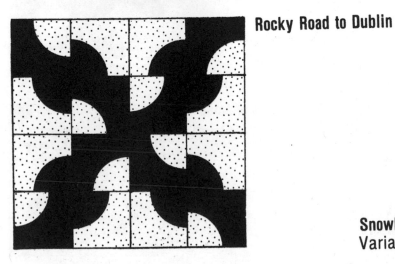

Snowball
Variation 4

Snowball Wreath

Steeplechase
Bows and Arrows

Strawberry
Full-Blown Tulip, Var. 1
Oriental Star, Var. 2

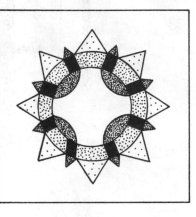

Spools
Always Friends
Friendship Chain

Turkey Tracks
Variation 1
Wandering Foot

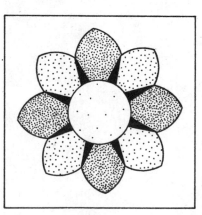

Star Flower   Variation 1
Golden Glow, Var. 1

Unnamed
Variation 1

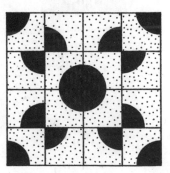

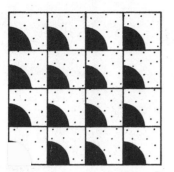

Unnamed Variation 2

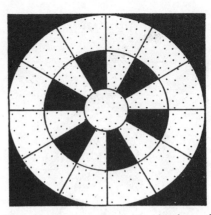

Wheel of Fortune Variation 4

Victoria's Crown

Wheel of Fortune Variation 5

Wheel of Chance
True Lover's Buggy Wheel

Wonder of the World

SUPPLEMENT

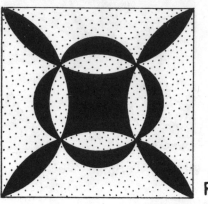

Reel

Combinations

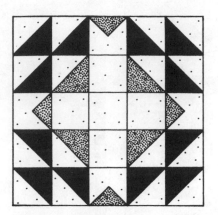

Album   Variation 1

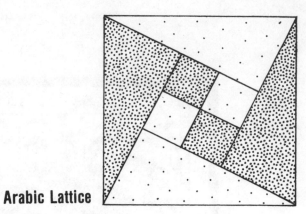

Arabic Lattice

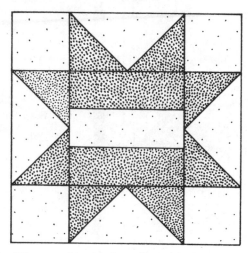

Album   Variation 2

Arrowheads   Variation 1

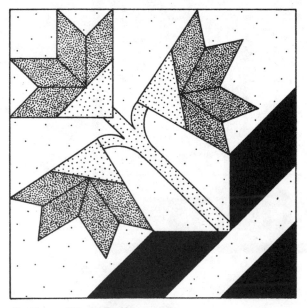

Antique Shop Tulip
Double Tulip

Aunt Sukey's Choice
Puss 'n' Boots

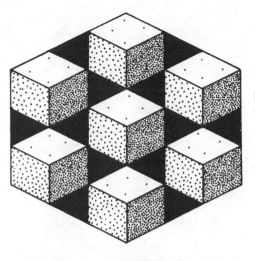

Baby Blocks
Variation 2

Baskets

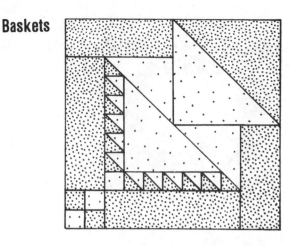

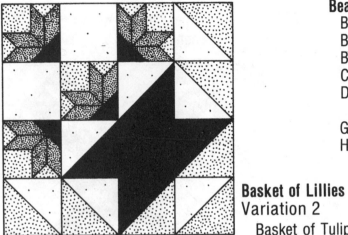

Bear Tracks Variation 1
Bear's Foot
Bear's Paw, Var. 3
Bear's Track, Var. 1
Cross and Crown, Var. 3
Duck's Foot in the Mud,
Var. 2
Goose Tracks, Var. 1
Hand of Friendship, Var. 2

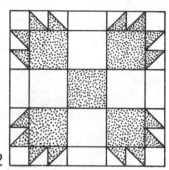

Illinois Turkey Track
Lily Design

Basket of Lillies
Variation 2
Basket of Tulips, Var. 2

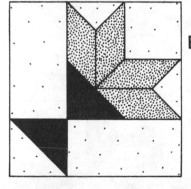

Basket of Scraps
Cactus Basket, Var. 2
Desert Rose, Var. 2
Texas Rose, Var. 2
Texas Treasure, Var. 2

Bear Tracks
Variation 2
Bear's Track, Var. 2

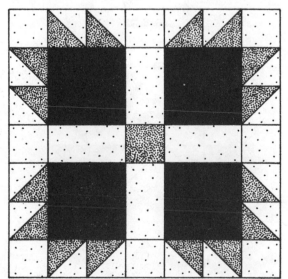

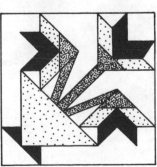

Basket of Tulips
Variation 1
Basket of Lilies, Var. 1

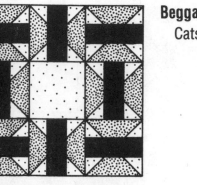

Beggar's Block
Cats and Mice, Var. 2

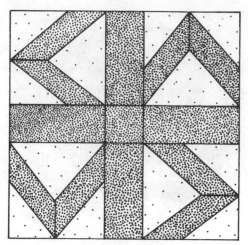

Bow Knot
Farmer's Puzzle
Swastika, Var. 1

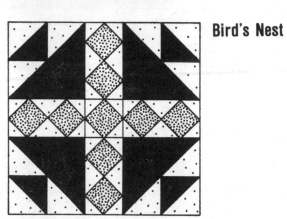

Bird's Nest

Blackford's Beauty

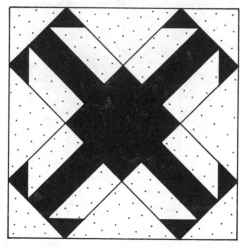

Boxed Ts

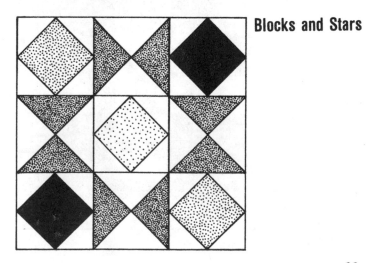

Blocks and Stars

Braced Star

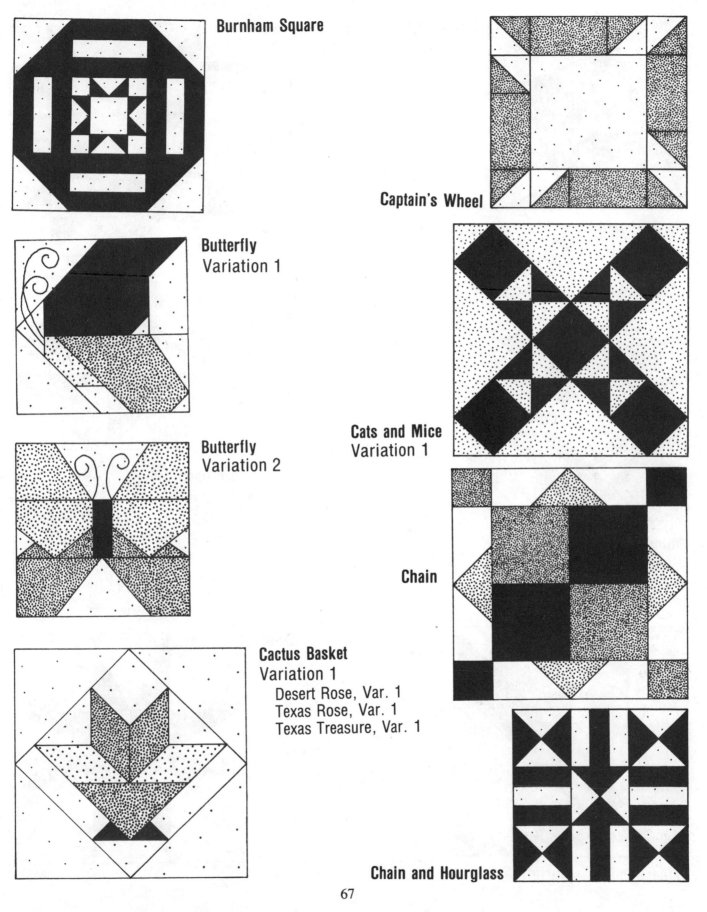

Burnham Square

Captain's Wheel

Butterfly
Variation 1

Cats and Mice
Variation 1

Butterfly
Variation 2

Chain

Cactus Basket
Variation 1
    Desert Rose, Var. 1
    Texas Rose, Var. 1
    Texas Treasure, Var. 1

Chain and Hourglass

67

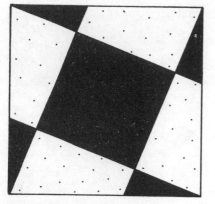

Checkerboard Skew

Christmas Star
Variation 2

Children of Israel

Churn Dash Variation 1
Lover's Knot
Monkey Wrench, Var. 1

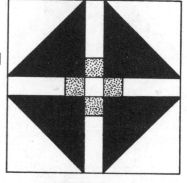

Churn Dash
Variation 2

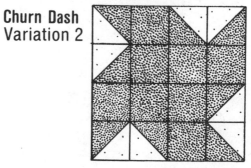

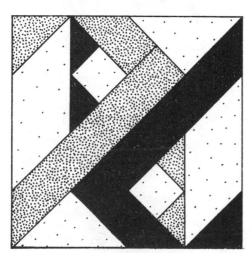

Chinese Puzzle Variation 1

Claws

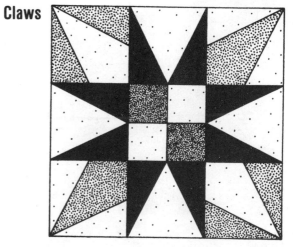

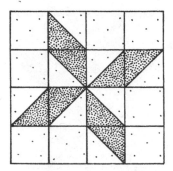

Clay's Choice
  Harry's Star
  Henry of the West
  Jackson's Star, Var. 2
  Star of the West, Var. 3

Crazy Ann   Variation 2

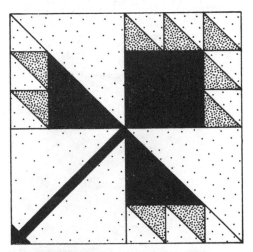

Clover Blossom
  English Ivy

Crazy House

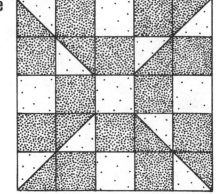

Combination Star
  Ornate Star

Cross and Crown
Variation 1

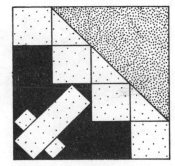

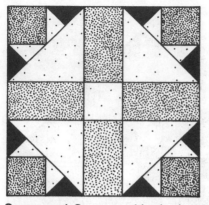

Cross and Crown Variation 4

Crow Foot
Devil's Claws,
Var. 2

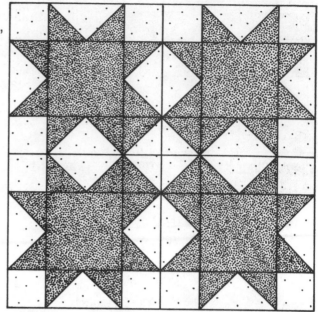

Cross Upon a Cross

Cross and Crown, Var. 2
Crown and Cross
Crowned Cross, Var. 1
Golgotha, Var. 2
Three Crosses, Var. 2

Crown and Thorns
Crown of Thorns
Georgetown Circle, Var. 1
Memory Wreath, Var. 1
Single Wedding Ring,
Var. 1

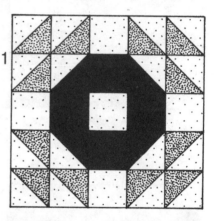

Crow's Foot
Variation 4

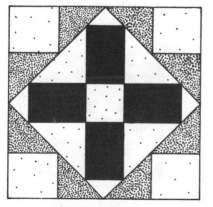

Cross Within a Cross

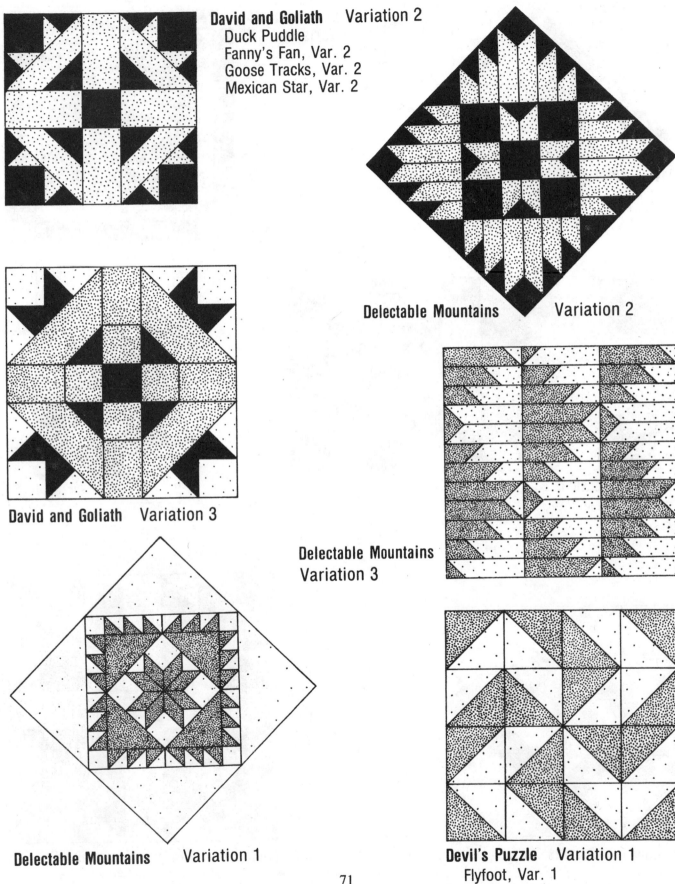

David and Goliath   Variation 2
Duck Puddle
Fanny's Fan, Var. 2
Goose Tracks, Var. 2
Mexican Star, Var. 2

Delectable Mountains   Variation 2

David and Goliath   Variation 3

Delectable Mountains
Variation 3

Delectable Mountains   Variation 1

Devil's Puzzle   Variation 1
Flyfoot, Var. 1

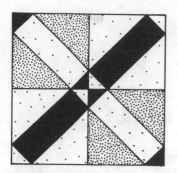

Devil's Puzzle Variation 2
Flyfoot, Var. 2

Double Square
Variation 1

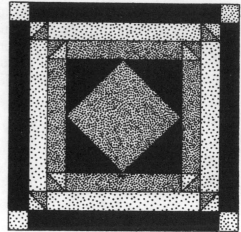

Dogwood Blossoms

Double X Variation 1

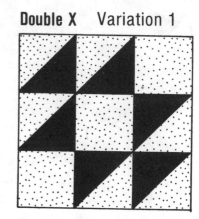

Domino and Squares

Dove in the Window Variation 2

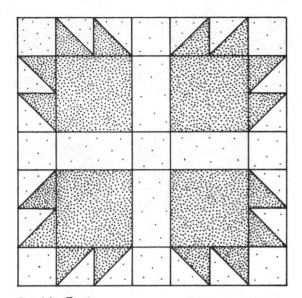

Duck's Foot

Duck's Foot in the Mud
Variation 1
   Bear's Paw, Var. 1
   Crow's Foot, Var. 1
   Hand of Friendship, Var. 1

Dusty Miller

Dutch Mill

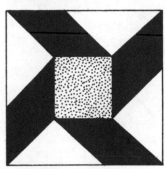

Eccentric Star
Variation 1

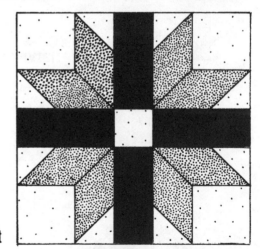

E-Z Quilt

Fannie's Fan
Variation 1

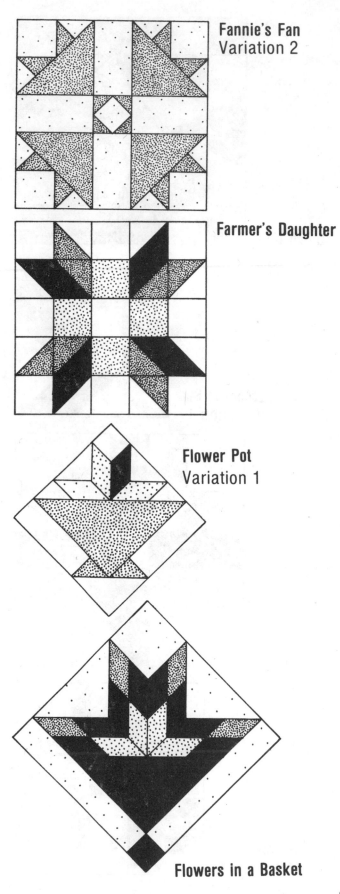

**Fannie's Fan
Variation 2**

Farmer's Daughter

**Flower Pot
Variation 1**

Flowers in a Basket

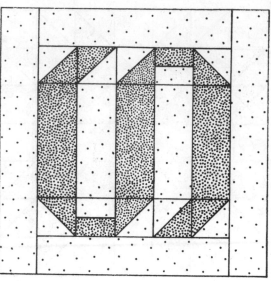

Flowing Ribbon

Flying Clouds   Variation 1
Four Frogs

**Flying Clouds
Variation 2**

Four Little Baskets

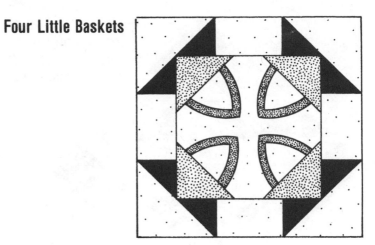

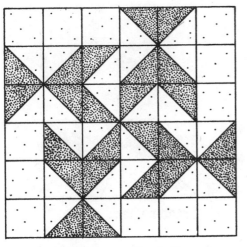

Flying Dutchman   Variation 1

Friendship Knot

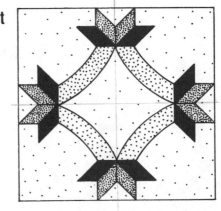

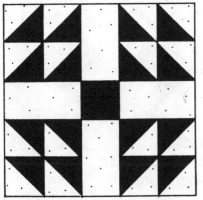

Flying Geese   Variation 2
Handy Andy, Var. 6

Four Darts
   Bull's Eye
   David and Goliath, Var. 1
   Doe and Darts
   Flying Darts

Garden of Eden   Variation 1

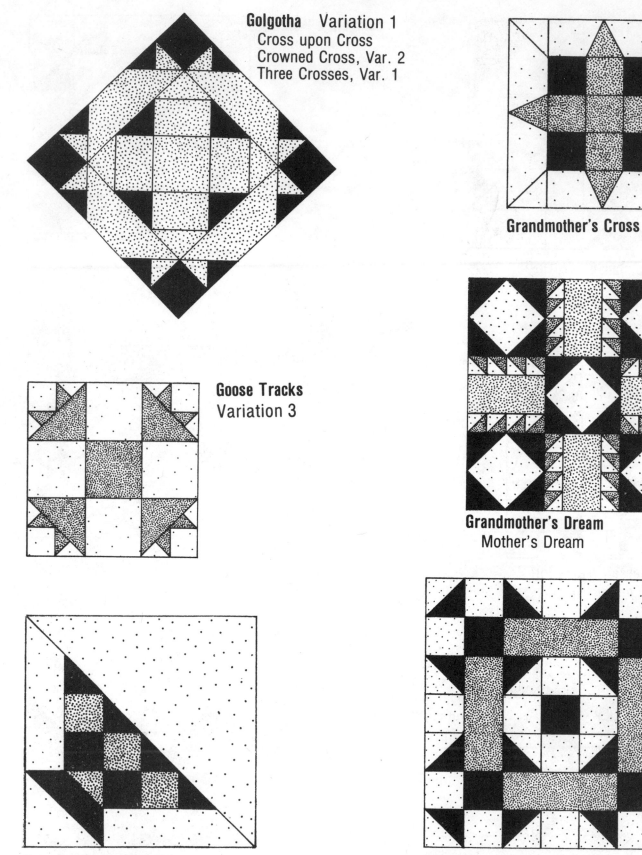

Golgotha Variation 1
Cross upon Cross
Crowned Cross, Var. 2
Three Crosses, Var. 1

Grandmother's Cross

Goose Tracks
Variation 3

Grandmother's Dream
Mother's Dream

Grandmother's Basket

Greek Cross Variation 2

76

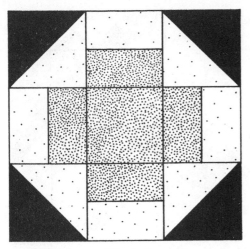

Greek Cross Variation 3
  Grecian
  Grecian Design

Handy Andy Variation 2

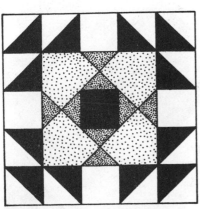

Handy Andy Variation 3

Hayes' Corner

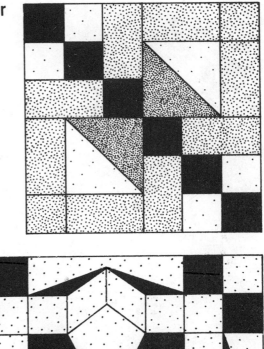

Heart's Desire

Hen and Chickens
Variation 2

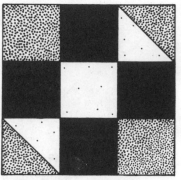

Hourglass Variation 1

Indian Hatchet
Variation 2

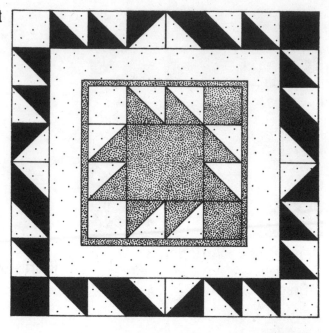

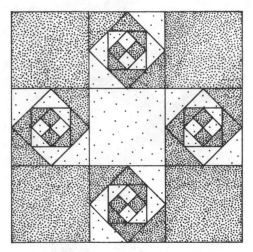

Indiana Puzzle
　Monkey Wrench, Var. 3

Indian Meadows Variation 1
　Mountain Meadows
　Queen Charlotte's Crown,
　　Var. 1

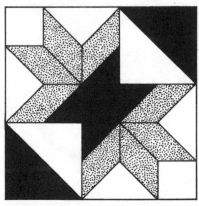

Irish Chain
Variation 1

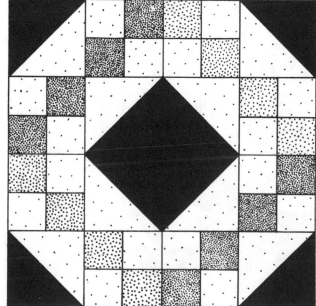

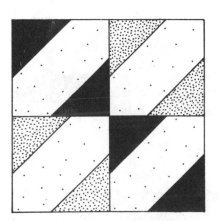

Indian Hatchet Variation 1

Jack in the Box
Whirligig, Var. 1

Joseph's Coat   Variation 1
Scrap-Bag

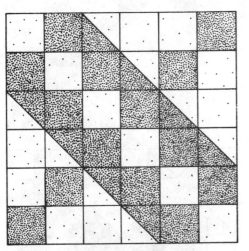

Jacob's Ladder   Variation 1

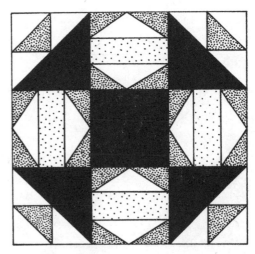

Joseph's Coat
Mollie's Choice   Variation 2

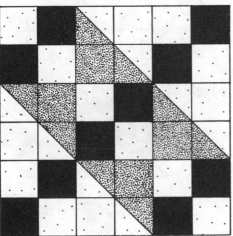

Jacob's Ladder   Variation 2
Road to California, Var. 1
Rocky Road to California
Stepping Stones, Var. 1
Tail of Benjamin's Kite
Trail of the Covered Wagon
Underground Railroad
Wagon Tracks

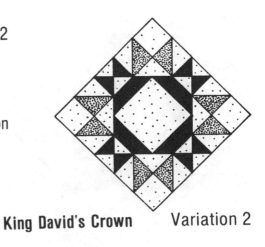

King David's Crown   Variation 2

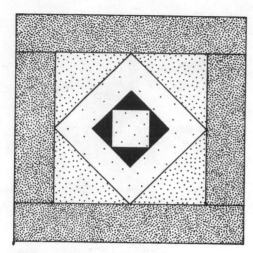

King's Crown Variation 1

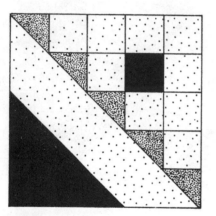

King's Crown Variation 2
Greek Cross, Var. 1

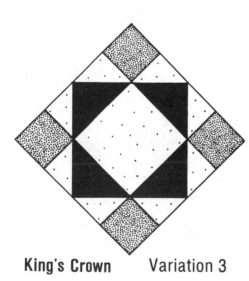

King's Crown Variation 3

Ladies' Delight

Leapfrog

Lily

Lily of the Field

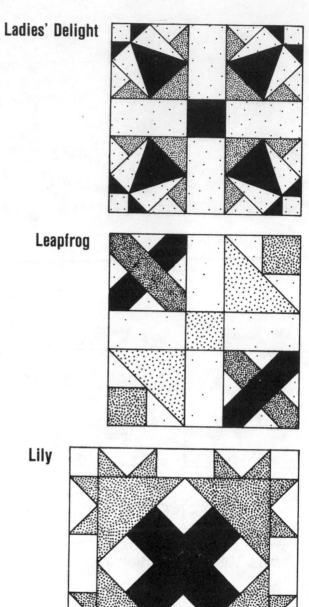

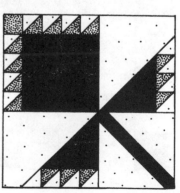

Little Giant

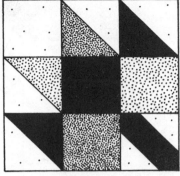

**Maple Leaf
Variation 2**
  Palm Leaf, Var. 2
  Poplar Leaf

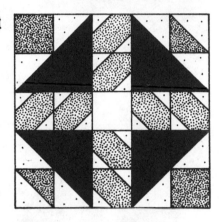

Mare's Nest

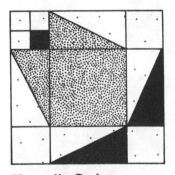

Magnolia Bud

Mary Tenney Gray Travel Club Patch

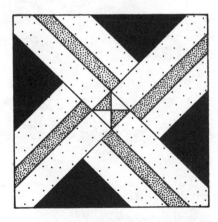

Maple Leaf   Variation 1

Memory Block

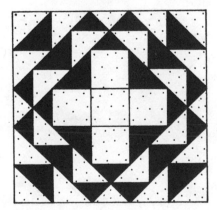

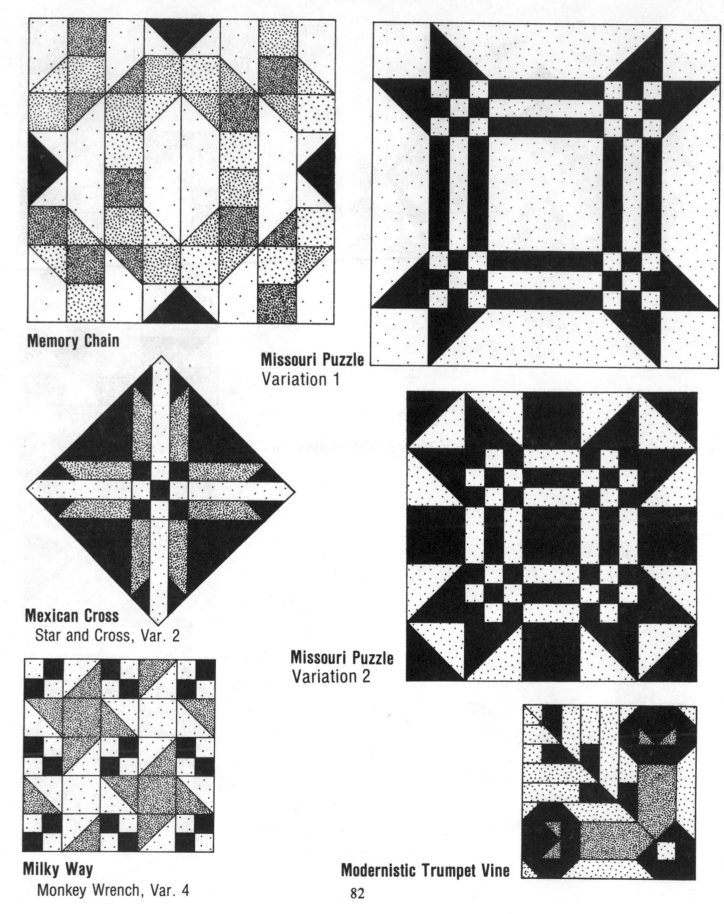

Memory Chain

Missouri Puzzle
Variation 1

Mexican Cross
Star and Cross, Var. 2

Missouri Puzzle
Variation 2

Milky Way
Monkey Wrench, Var. 4

Modernistic Trumpet Vine

Mother's Fancy Star

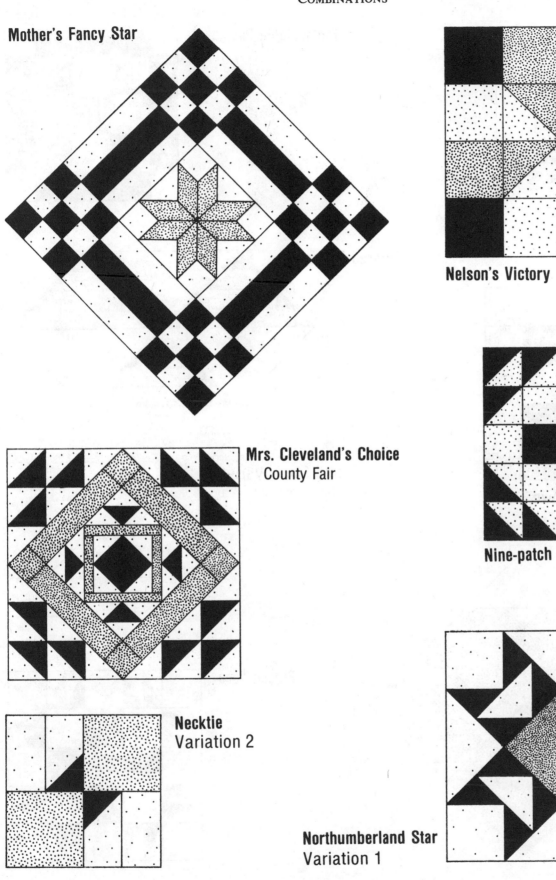

Nelson's Victory

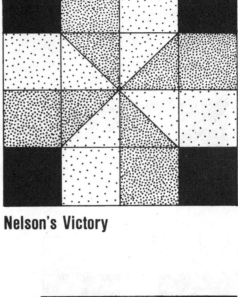

Mrs. Cleveland's Choice
County Fair

Nine-patch   Variation 2

Necktie
Variation 2

Northumberland Star
Variation 1

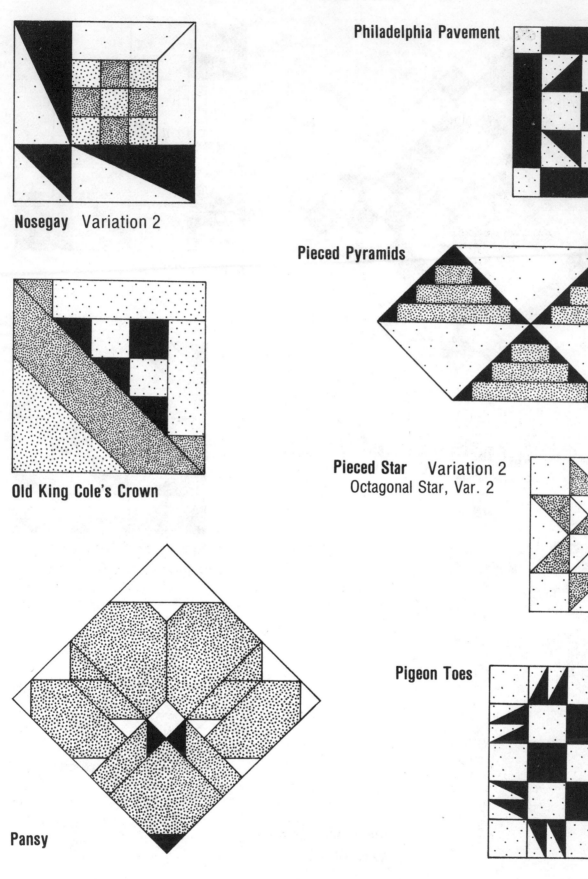

Philadelphia Pavement

Nosegay Variation 2

Pieced Pyramids

Old King Cole's Crown

Pieced Star Variation 2
Octagonal Star, Var. 2

Pigeon Toes

Pansy

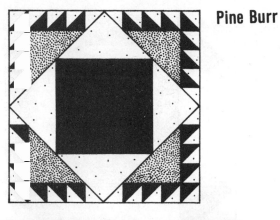

Pine Burr

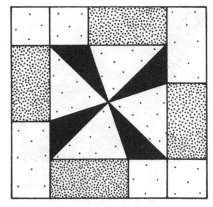

Pinwheel Skew

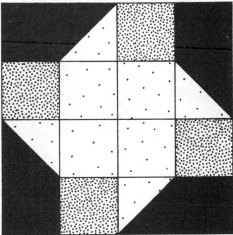

Pinwheel Variation 2
   Crow's Foot, Var. 2
   Fan Mill, Var. 2
   Flutter Wheels, Var. 2
   Fly, Var. 2
   Foot
   Kathy's Ramble, Var. 2
   Sugar Bowl, Var. 2

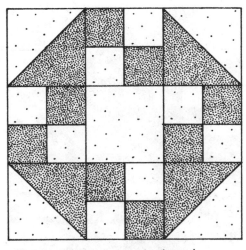

Prairie Queen Variation 1

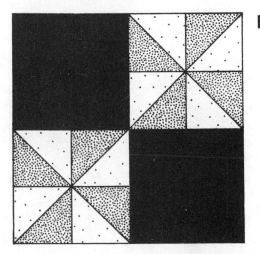

Pinwheels

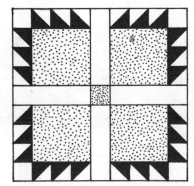

Premium Star

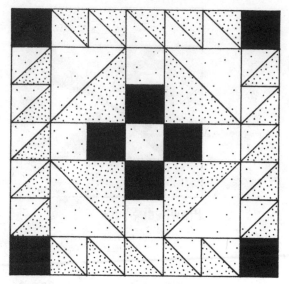

Prickly Pear Variation 1

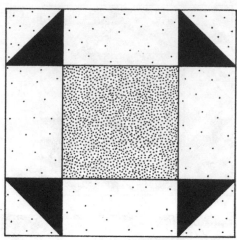

Puss in the Corner
Variation 1
    Kitty Corner, Var. 2
    Tic Tac Toe, Var. 2

Primrose Path

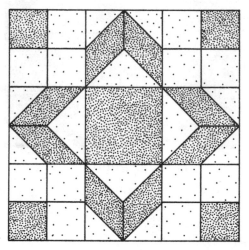

Puss in the Corner
Variation 2
    Puss in Boots

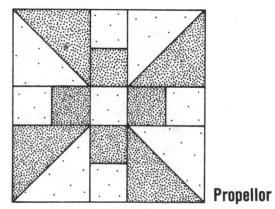

Propellor

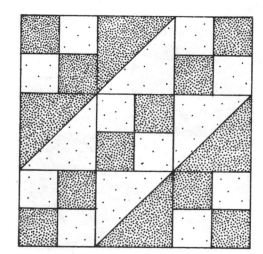

Railroad

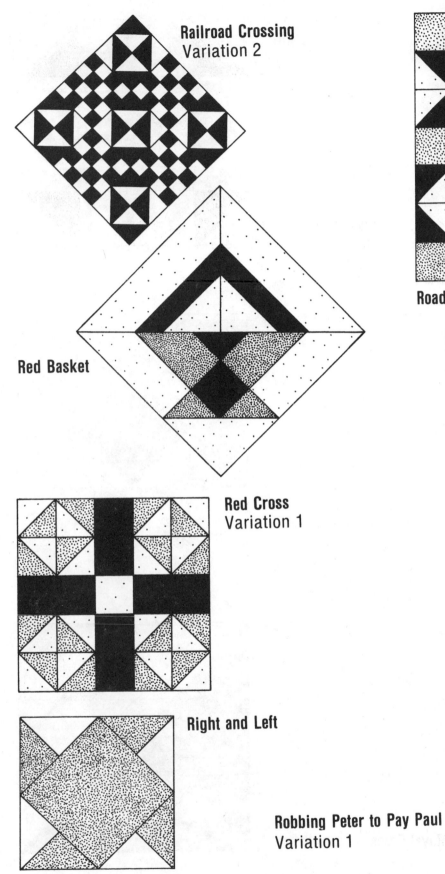

Railroad Crossing
Variation 2

Red Basket

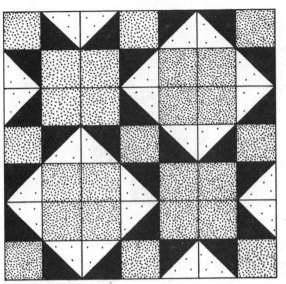

Road to California   Variation 3

Road to California   Variation 4

Red Cross
Variation 1

Right and Left

Robbing Peter to Pay Paul
Variation 1

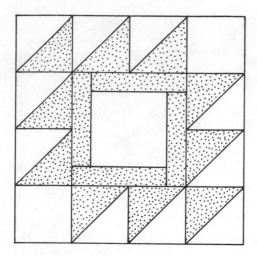

Rocky Mountain Puzzle

Sawtooth
Variation 3

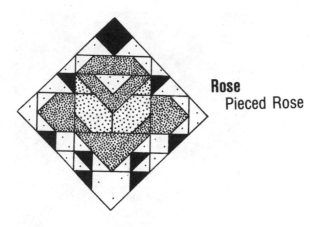

Rose
Pieced Rose

Secret Drawer

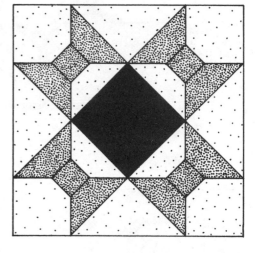

Royal Cross

Shadows

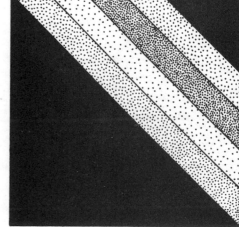

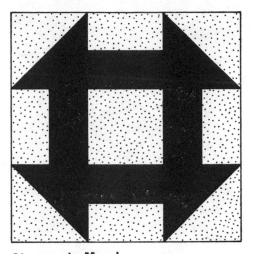

Sherman's March
Barn Door
Double Monkey Wrench
Hole in the Barn Door
Lincoln's Platform
Love Knot
Monkey Wrench, Var. 2
Quail's Nest

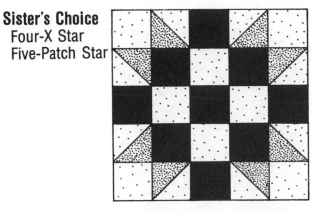

Sister's Choice
Four-X Star
Five-Patch Star

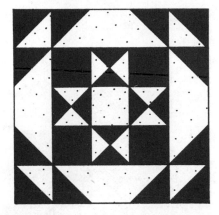

Square and a Half

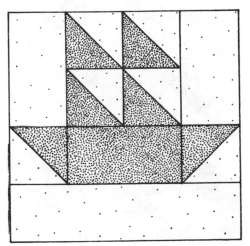

Ship

Square Within Squares

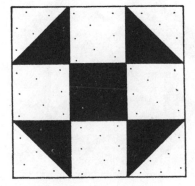

Shoofly Variation 1
Chinese Coin
Grandmother's Choice, Var. 2
Star Spangled Banner

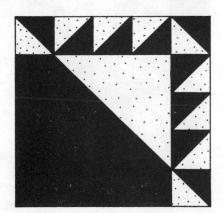

Star of Hope
Variation 1

89

 **Starry Lane**

 **Swing in the Center**

 **Stepping Stones**

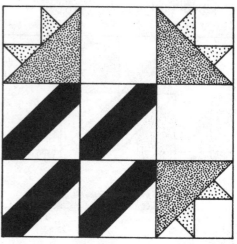 **Tassal Point**

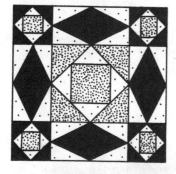 **Storm at Sea** Variation 2
Rolling Stone, Var. 1

T-Blocks Variation 2

 **Suspension Bridge**

Tea Basket

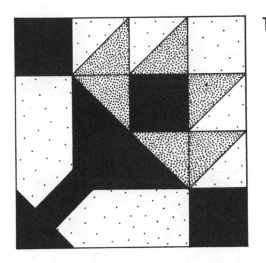

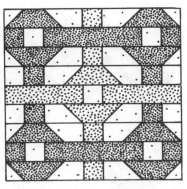

Tile Puzzle   Variation 2

Thelma's Choice

Toad in the Puddle   Variation 1

Toad in the Puddle
Variation 2
   Double Square, Var. 2
   Jack in the Pulpit

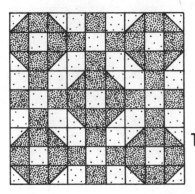

Tile Puzzle   Variation 1
Improved Nine-Patch, Var. 2
Puzzled Tile

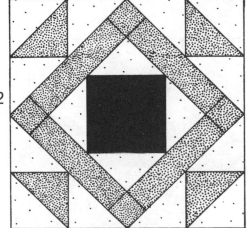

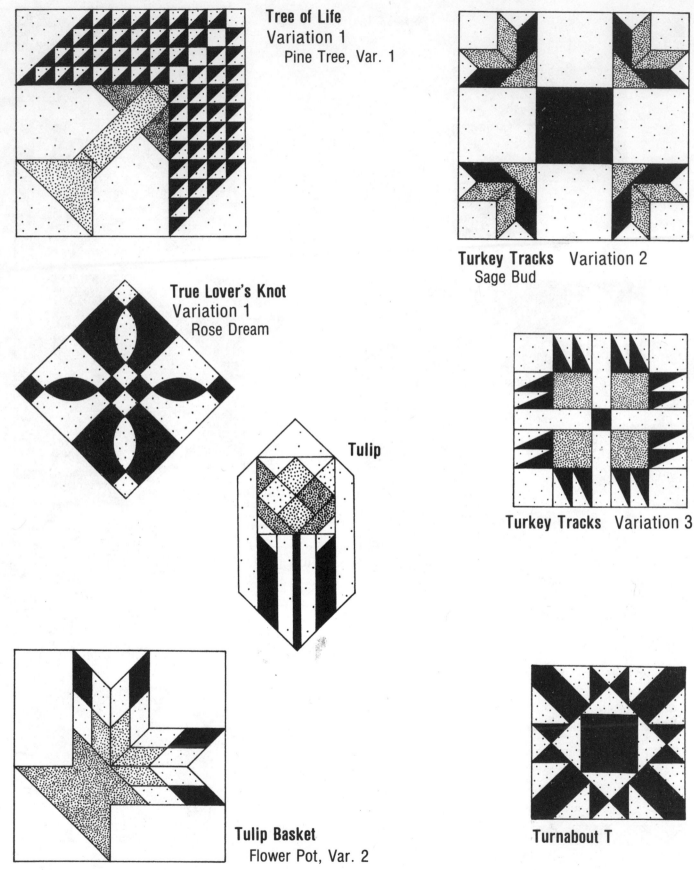

Tree of Life
Variation 1
Pine Tree, Var. 1

Turkey Tracks Variation 2
Sage Bud

True Lover's Knot
Variation 1
Rose Dream

Tulip

Turkey Tracks Variation 3

Tulip Basket
Flower Pot, Var. 2

Turnabout T

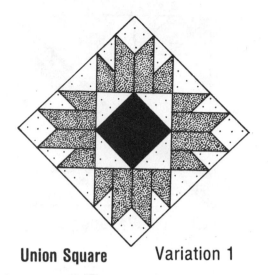

Union Square Variation 1

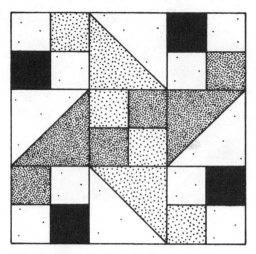

Water Wheel Variation 3

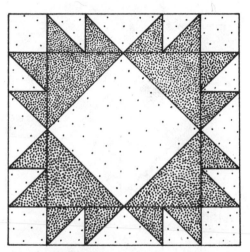

Union Square Variation 2

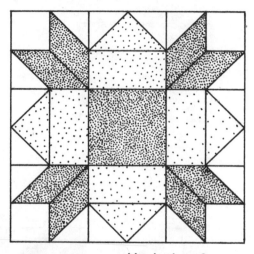

Weather Vane Variation 2

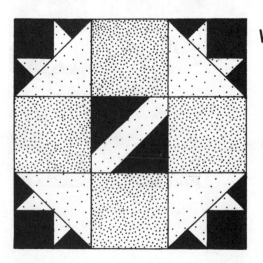

W.C.T.U.

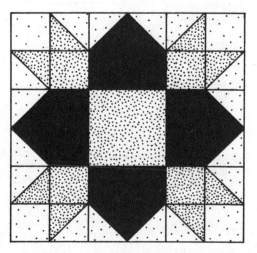

Weather Vane
Variation 3

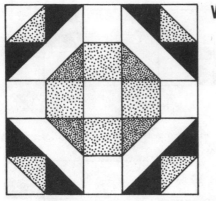

Wedding Rings

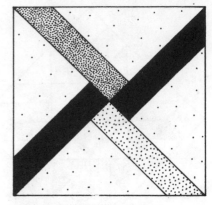

Windmill Variation 3

White Cross

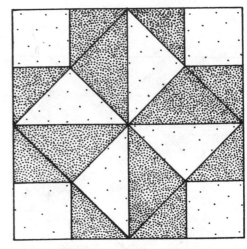

Windmill Variation 5

Wild Goose Chase Variation 3

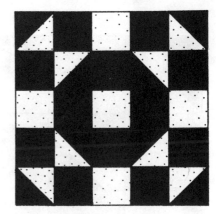

Wishing Ring

World's Fair Variation 1

X-Quartet

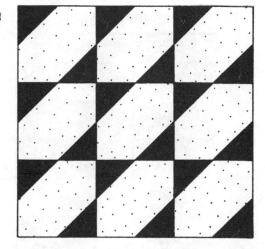

X-Quisite

World's Fair Variation 2

Wrench

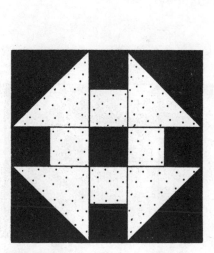

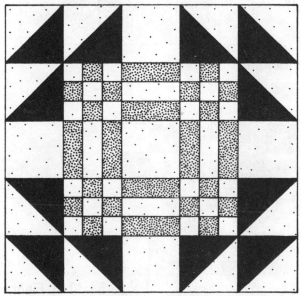

Young Man's Fancy
Goose in the Pond, Var. 2
Mrs. Wolf's Red Beauty

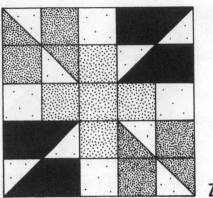

Z-Cross

Grandmother's Choice
Variation 1

SUPPLEMENT

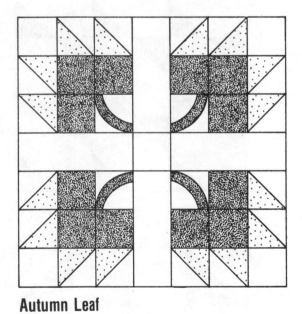

Nosegay

Autumn Leaf

St. George's Cross

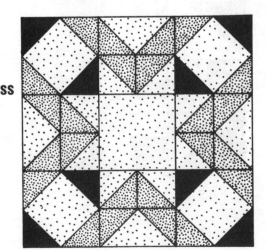

54-40 or Fight

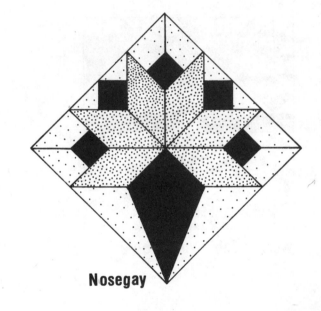

96

Squares

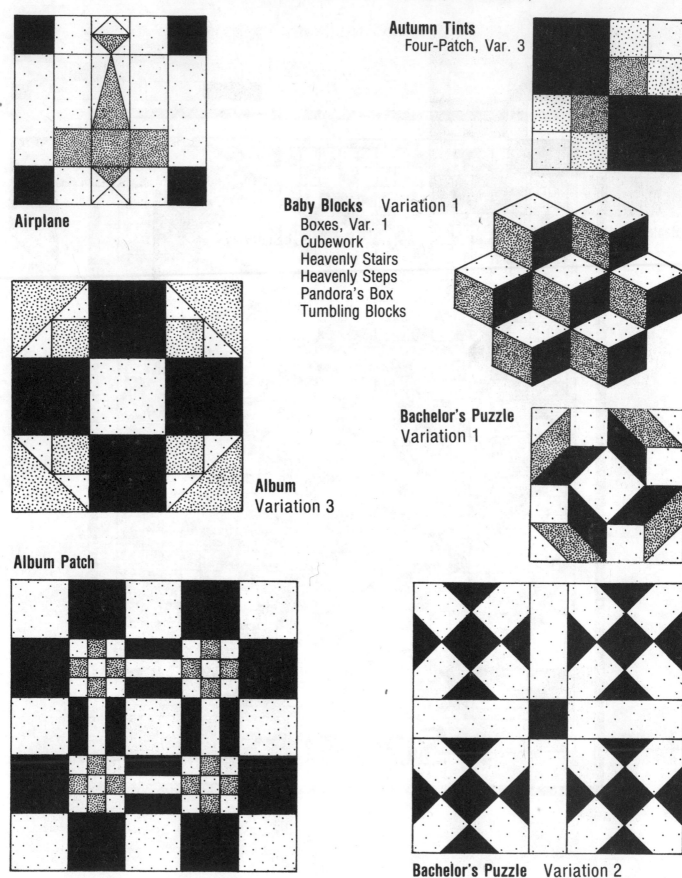

Autumn Tints
Four-Patch, Var. 3

Airplane

Baby Blocks Variation 1
  Boxes, Var. 1
  Cubework
  Heavenly Stairs
  Heavenly Steps
  Pandora's Box
  Tumbling Blocks

Album
Variation 3

Bachelor's Puzzle
Variation 1

Album Patch

Bachelor's Puzzle Variation 2

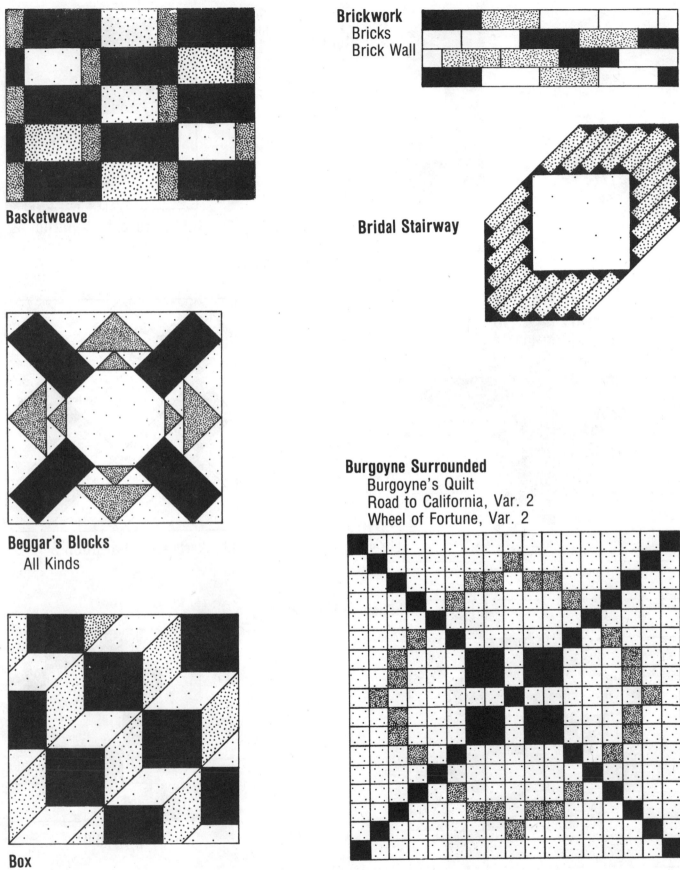

Basketweave

Brickwork
Bricks
Brick Wall

Bridal Stairway

Beggar's Blocks
All Kinds

Burgoyne Surrounded
Burgoyne's Quilt
Road to California, Var. 2
Wheel of Fortune, Var. 2

Box

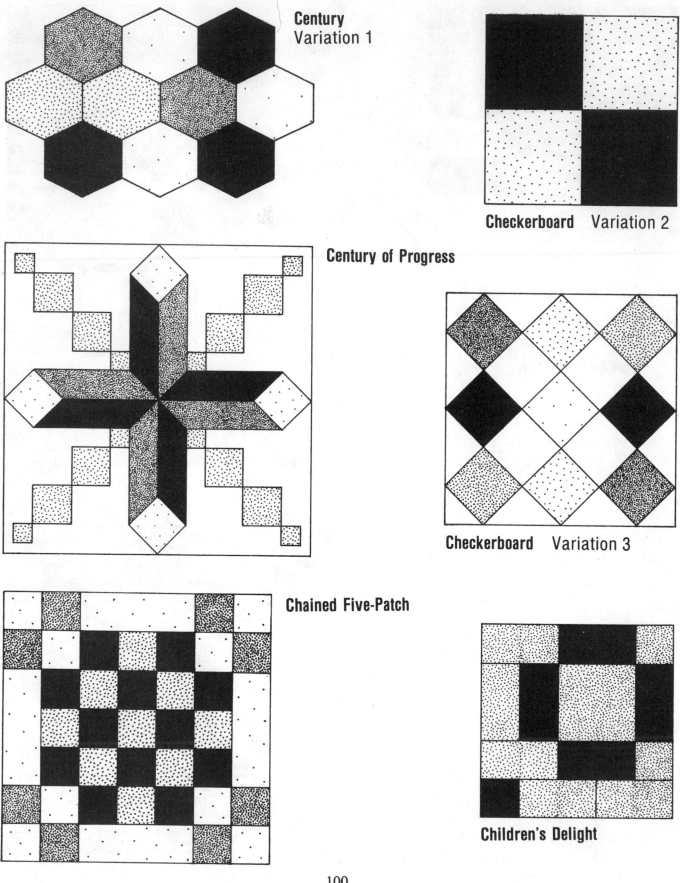

Century
Variation 1

Checkerboard   Variation 2

Century of Progress

Checkerboard   Variation 3

Chained Five-Patch

Children's Delight

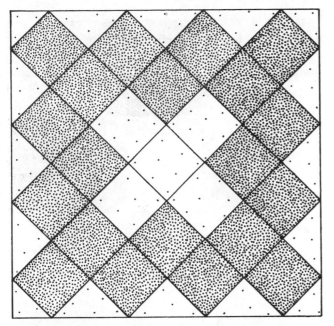

Christian Cross

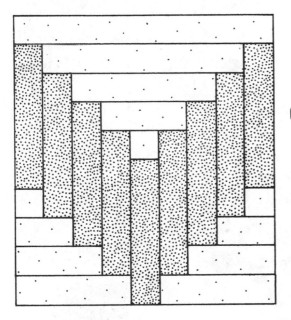

Coarsewoven
Variation 2
Finewoven, Var. 2

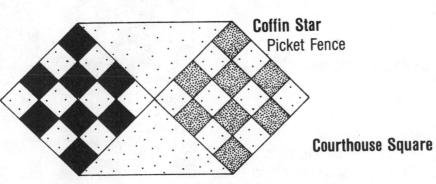

Coffin Star
Picket Fence

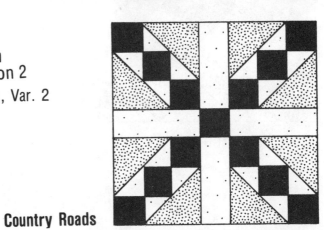

Contrary Wife

Corner Posts

Country Roads

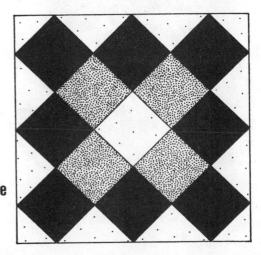

Courthouse Square

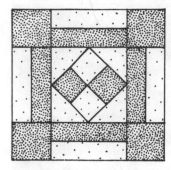

Coxey's Camp

Domino Variation 1

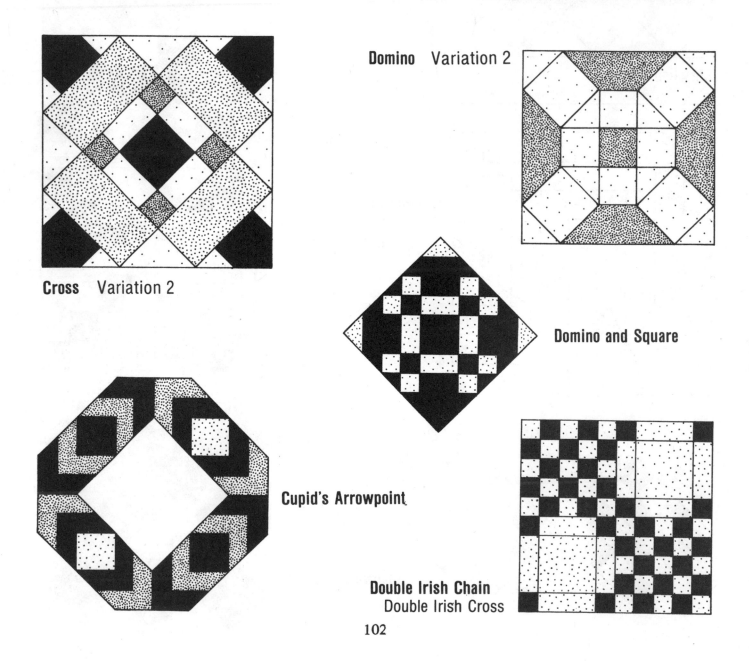

Cross Variation 2

Domino Variation 2

Domino and Square

Cupid's Arrowpoint

Double Irish Chain
Double Irish Cross

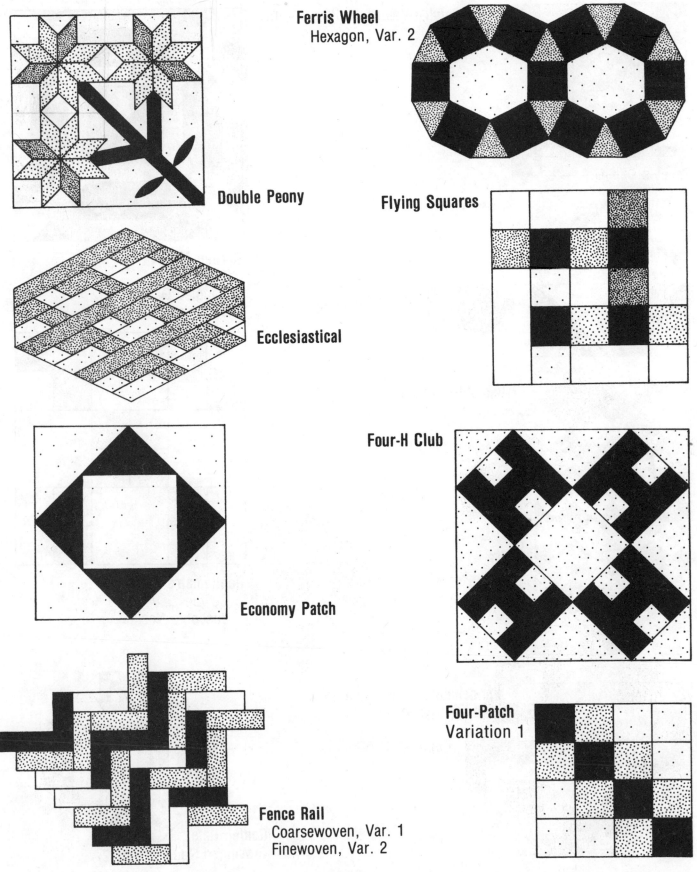

Ferris Wheel
Hexagon, Var. 2

Double Peony

Flying Squares

Ecclesiastical

Four-H Club

Economy Patch

Four-Patch
Variation 1

Fence Rail
Coarsewoven, Var. 1
Finewoven, Var. 2

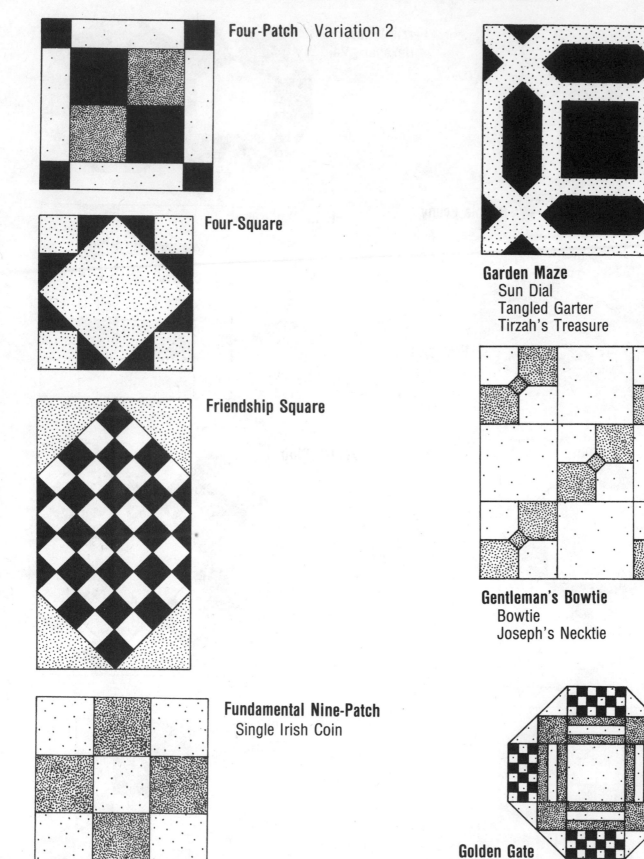

Four-Patch Variation 2

Four-Square

Friendship Square

Fundamental Nine-Patch
Single Irish Coin

Garden Maze
Sun Dial
Tangled Garter
Tirzah's Treasure

Gentleman's Bowtie
Bowtie
Joseph's Necktie

Golden Gate
Winged Square, Var. 2

Golden Glow Variation 2

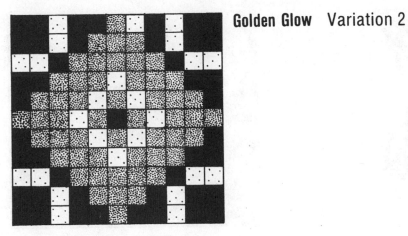

Granny's Flower Garden

Grandma's Red and White

Grandmother's Flower Garden

Flower Garden   Rainbow Tile
French Bouquet   Rosette
Grandma's Garden   Spider Web, Var. 1
Honeycomb, Var. 1
Job's Troubles, Var. 1
Martha Washington's Flower Garden
Mosaic

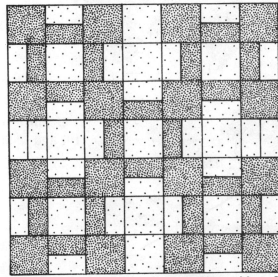

Hand

California Oakleaf   True Lover's Knot, Var. 2
Sassafras Leaf

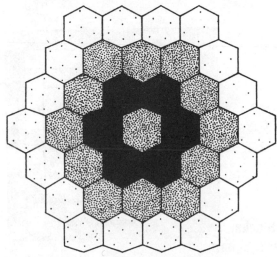

Hanging Diamond

105

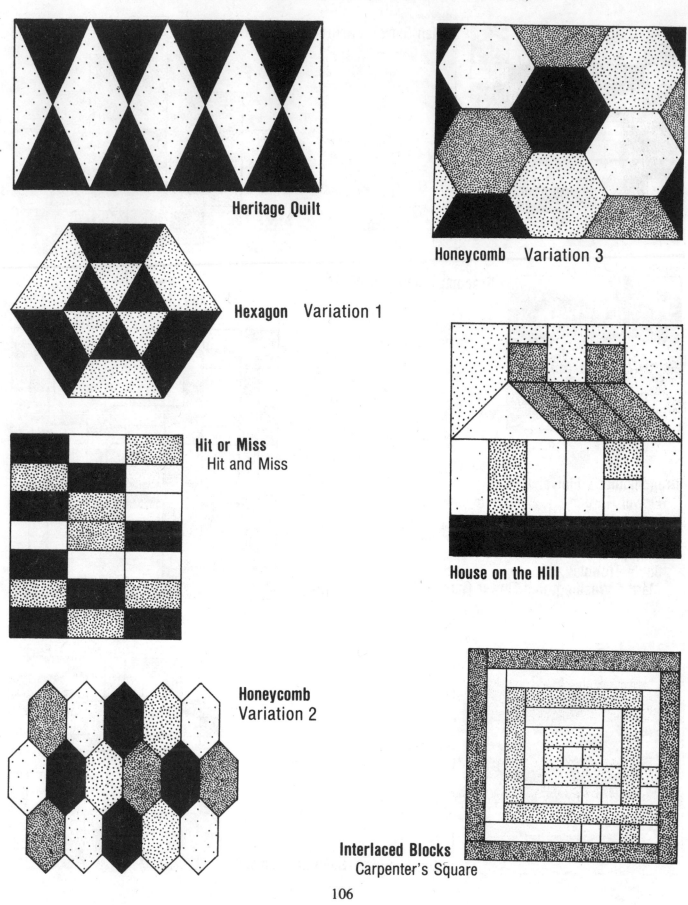

Heritage Quilt

Honeycomb   Variation 3

Hexagon   Variation 1

Hit or Miss
Hit and Miss

House on the Hill

Honeycomb
Variation 2

Interlaced Blocks
Carpenter's Square

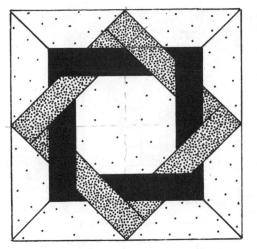

Interlocked Squares

Kansas Dugout

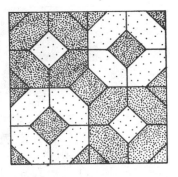

Kite's Tail

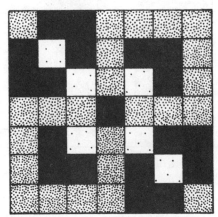

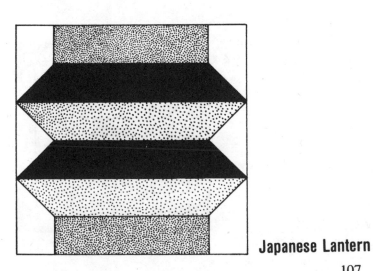

Irish Chain Variation 2
Double Nine-Patch

Leavenworth Nine-Patch

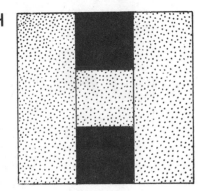

Letter H

Japanese Lantern

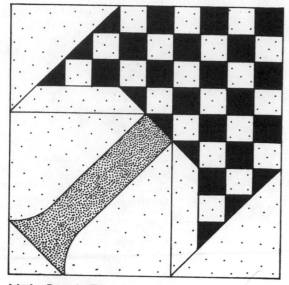

Little Beech Tree

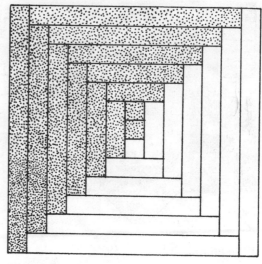

Log Cabin Variation 2
Courthouse Steps

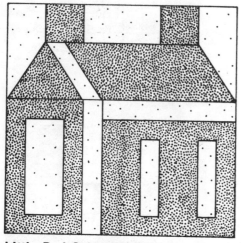

Little Red Schoolhouse

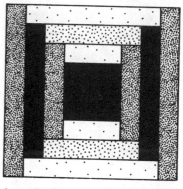

Log Cabin Variation 3

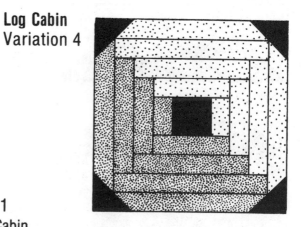

Log Cabin
Variation 4

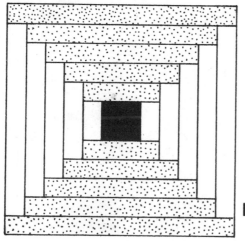

Log Cabin Variation 1
Old-Fashioned Log Cabin

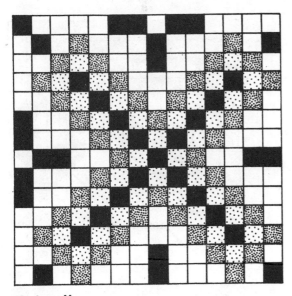

Madam X

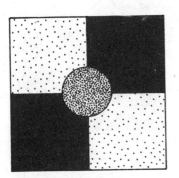

Necktie Variation 1

Nine-Patch Variation 1

Nine-Patch Variation 3

Nine-Patch Variation 4

Nine-Patch Chain

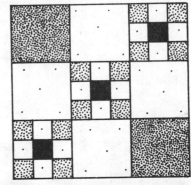

Octagon

109

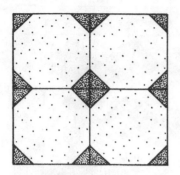

Octagons

Patience Corners

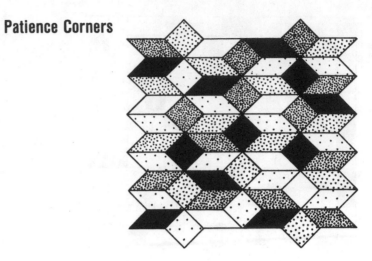

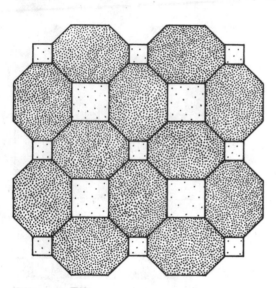

Octagon Tile

Peony

Patience Corner

Pineapple
Chestnut Burr
Church Steps
Maltese Cross, Var. 2

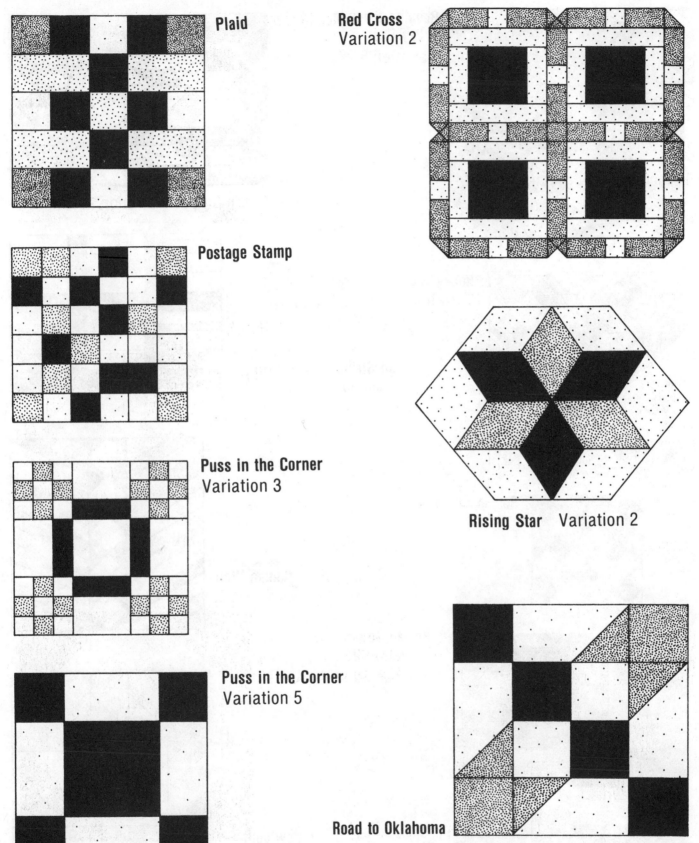

Plaid

Red Cross
Variation 2

Postage Stamp

Puss in the Corner
Variation 3

Rising Star   Variation 2

Puss in the Corner
Variation 5

Road to Oklahoma

New Four-Patch

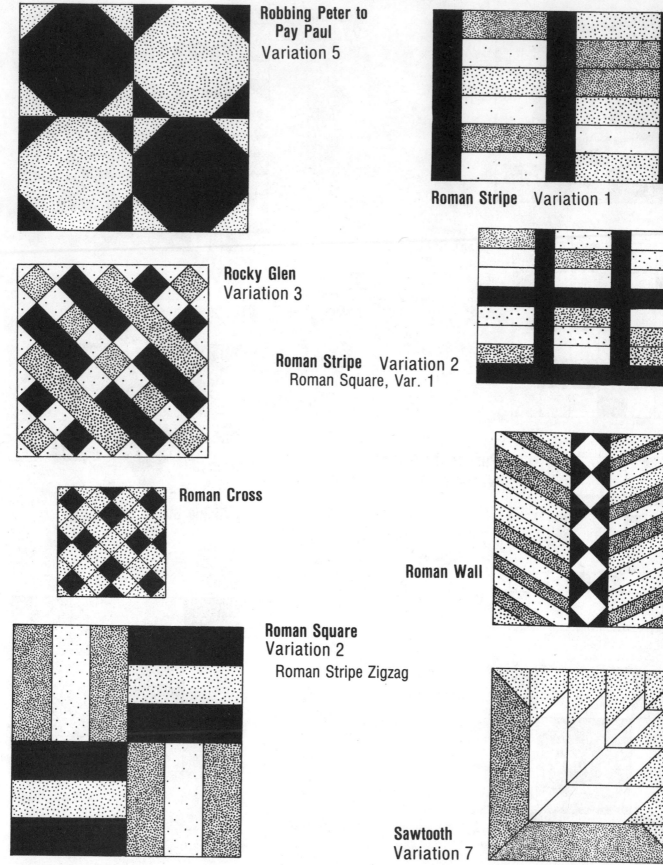

Robbing Peter to Pay Paul
Variation 5

Roman Stripe Variation 1

Rocky Glen
Variation 3

Roman Stripe Variation 2
Roman Square, Var. 1

Roman Cross

Roman Wall

Roman Square
Variation 2
Roman Stripe Zigzag

Sawtooth
Variation 7

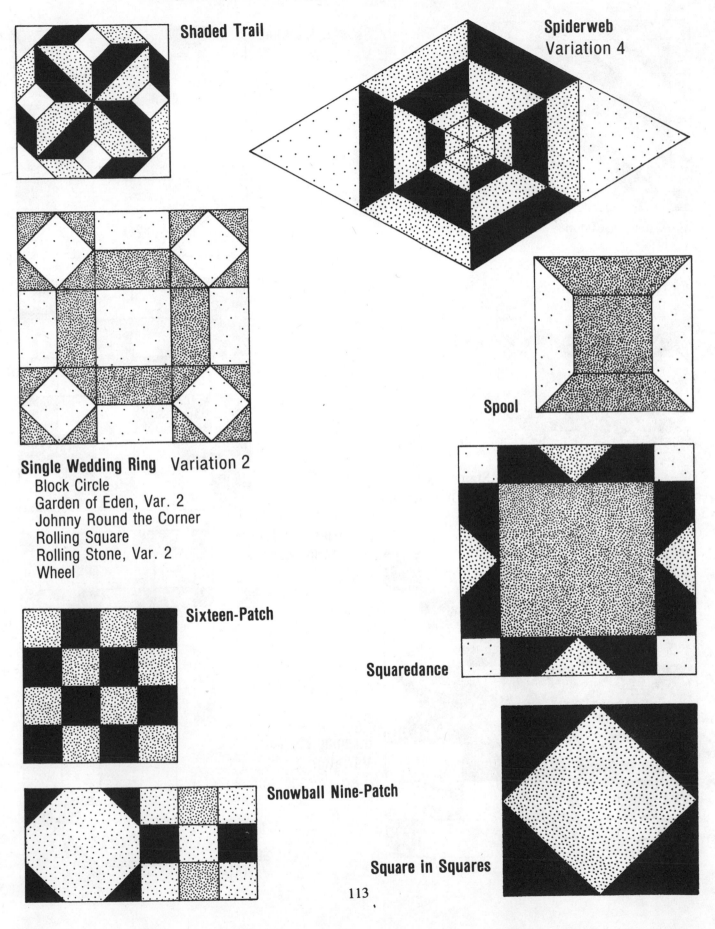

Shaded Trail

Spiderweb
Variation 4

Spool

Single Wedding Ring Variation 2
    Block Circle
    Garden of Eden, Var. 2
    Johnny Round the Corner
    Rolling Square
    Rolling Stone, Var. 2
    Wheel

Sixteen-Patch

Squaredance

Snowball Nine-Patch

Square in Squares

113

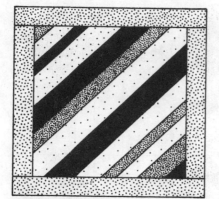

Square with Stripes

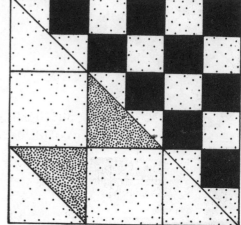

Steps to the Altar
Variation 2

Stained Glass
Church Window

Streak O'Lightning

Strips and Squares
Strip Squares

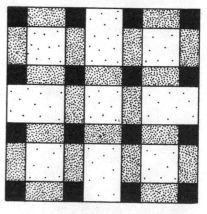

Stepping Stones
Variation 2
Arrowheads, Var. 2

Susannah
Variation 1

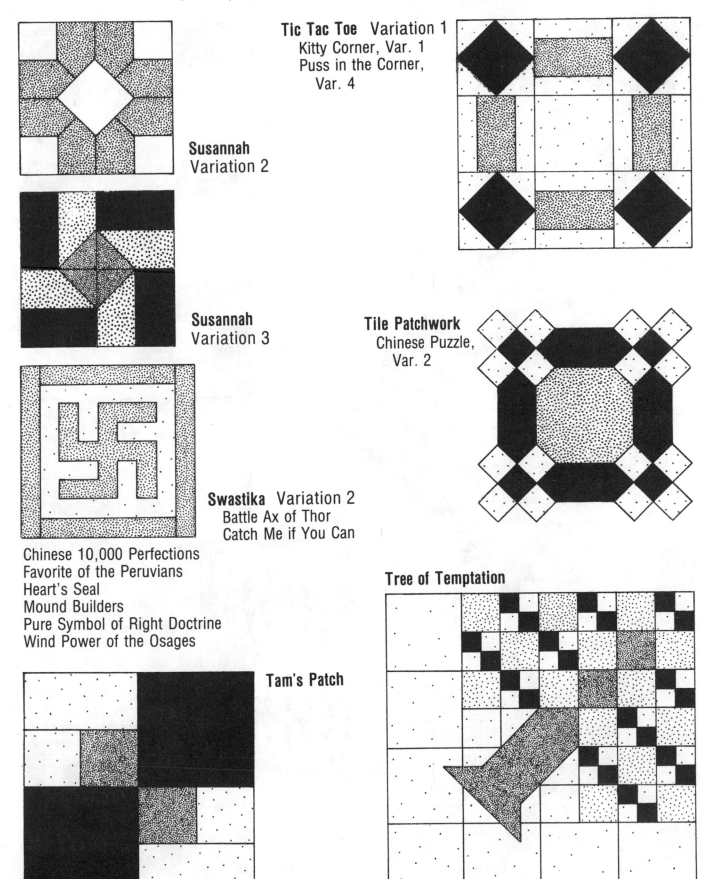

Tic Tac Toe Variation 1
Kitty Corner, Var. 1
Puss in the Corner,
Var. 4

Susannah
Variation 2

Susannah
Variation 3

Tile Patchwork
Chinese Puzzle,
Var. 2

Swastika Variation 2
Battle Ax of Thor
Catch Me if You Can

Chinese 10,000 Perfections
Favorite of the Peruvians
Heart's Seal
Mound Builders
Pure Symbol of Right Doctrine
Wind Power of the Osages

Tam's Patch

Tree of Temptation

115

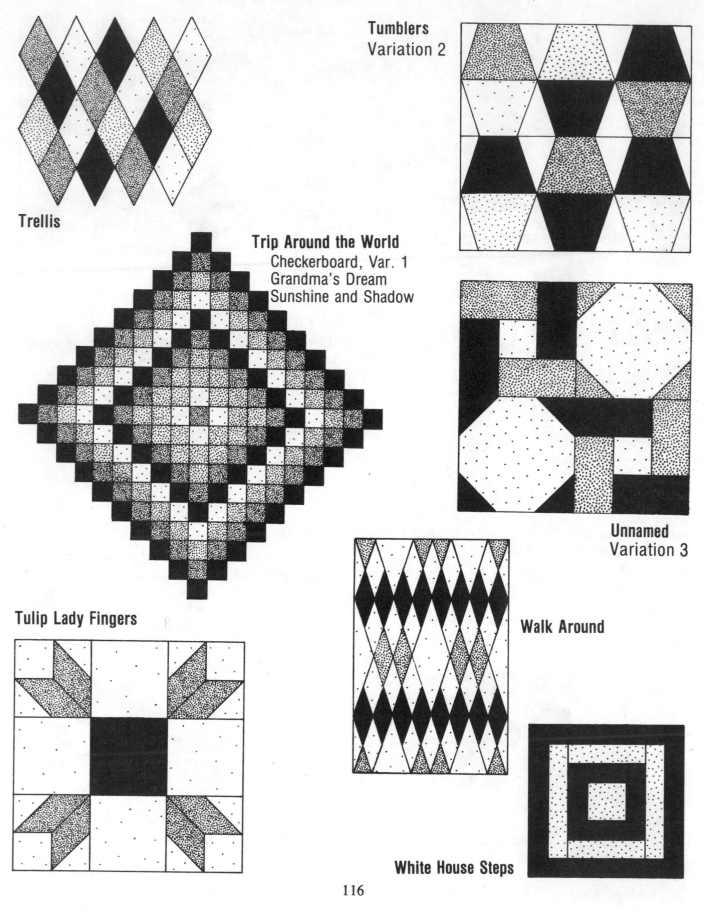

Tumblers
Variation 2

Trellis

Trip Around the World
Checkerboard, Var. 1
Grandma's Dream
Sunshine and Shadow

Unnamed
Variation 3

Walk Around

Tulip Lady Fingers

White House Steps

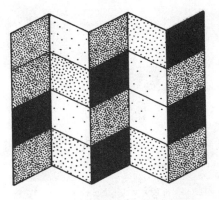

Zigzag
Variation 2
Snake Fence, Var. 2

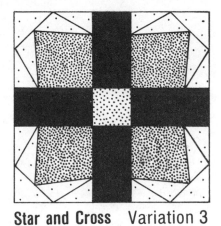

Star and Cross   Variation 3

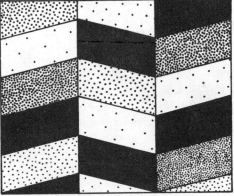

Zigzag
Variation 3

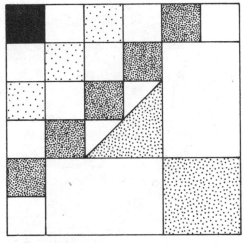

Steps to the Altar   Variation 1

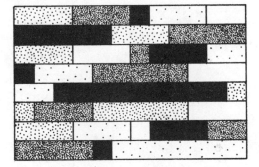

Zigzag Block

SUPPLEMENT

Flying Bats

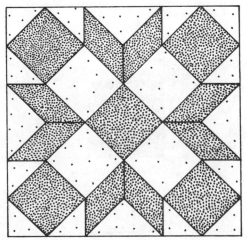

Swing in the Center
Variation 2

BIBLIOGRAPHY

Bicentennial Quilt Book, McCall's Needlework & Crafts, Editorial Director, Rosemary McMurtry, McCall Pattern Co., New York, 1975.

ERICSON, HELEN M., *Helen's Book of Basic Quiltmaking*, Groh Printing Co., Emporia, Kansas, 1973.

FINLEY, RUTH E., *Old Patchwork Quilts*, Charles T. Branford Co., Newton Centre, Mass., c. 1929, reprinted 1970.

The Foxfire Book, Editor, Eliot Wigginton, Anchor Books/Doubleday, Garden City, N.Y., 1972.

GRAFTON, CAROL BELANGER, *Traditional Patchwork Patterns*, Dover Publications, Inc., New York, 1974.

GREEN, SYLVIA, *Patchwork for Beginners*, Watson-Guptill Publications, New York, 1972.

GUTCHEON, BETH, *The Perfect Patchwork Primer*, Penguin Books Inc., Baltimore, 1973.

Heirloom Quilts, McCall's Needlework and Crafts, Editorial Director, Rosemary McMurtry, McCall Pattern Co., 1974.

HINSON, DOLORES, A., *A Quilter's Companion*, Arco Publishing, Inc., New York, 1973.

HOLSTEIN, JONATHAN, *American Pieced Quilts*, Viking Press, New York, 1972.

LARSEN, JUDITH LA BELLE & GULL, CAROL WAUGH, *The Patchwork Quilt Design & Coloring Book*, Butterick Publishing, New York, 1977.

LITHGOW, MARILYN, *Quiltmaking & Quiltmakers*, Funk & Wagnalls, New York, 1974.

MAHLER, CELINE BLANCHARD, *Once Upon a Quilt*, Van Nostrand Reinhold Co., New York, 1973.

The McCall's Book of Quilts, Editors of McCall's Needlework & Crafts Publications, Simon & Schuster/The McCall Pattern Company, New York, 1975.

McKIM, RUBY SHORT, *One Hundred and One Patchwork Patterns*, Dover Publications, Inc., New York, 1962.

Mountain Artizans, An Exhibition of Patchwork and Quilting, Museum of Art, Rhode Island School of Design, Providence, 1970.

Mrs. Danner's Fifth Quilt Book, Editor, Helen M. Ericson, Groh Printing Co., Emporia, Kansas, 1972.

Mrs. Danner's Quilts, Books 1 and 2 combined, Editor, Helen M. Ericson, Groh Printing Co., Emporia, Kansas, 1971.

Mrs. Danner's Quilts, Books 3 and 4 combined, Editor, Helen M. Ericson, Groh Printing Co., Emporia, Kansas, 1973.

ORLOFSKY, PATSY & MYRON, *Quilts in America*, McGraw-Hill Book Co., New York, 1974.

PETO, FLORENCE, *Quilts & Coverlets*, Chanticleer Press, New York, 1949.

Quilter's Newsletter Magazine, Editor-Bonnie Leman, Leman Publications, Inc., Denver.

Quilt World, Editor-Barbara Hall Pedersen.

150 Years of American Quilts, The University of Kansas Museum of Art, Lawrence, Kansas, 1973.

INDEX